NOT COOL

NOT *Cool*

THE HIPSTER ELITE AND
THEIR WAR ON YOU

GREG
GUTFELD

CROWN
FORUM
NEW YORK

Published in the United States by Crown Forum,
an imprint of the Crown Publishing Group,
a division of Random House LLC,
a Penguin Random House Company, New York.
www.crownpublishing.com

CROWN FORUM with colophon is a registered trademark
of Random House LLC.

Originally published in hardcover in the United States
by Crown Forum, an imprint of the Crown Publishing Group,
a division of Random House LLC, New York, in 2014.

Library of Congress Cataloging-in-Publication Data
Gutfeld, Greg.
    Not cool : the hipster elite and their war on you /
Greg Gutfeld.
        pages cm
        1. Conduct of life—Humor. 2. Elite (Social sciences)—
Humor. I. Title.
PN6231.C6142G88 2014
818'.602—dc23   2013050828

ISBN 978-0-8041-3855-0
eBook ISBN 978-0-8041-3854-3

Cover design by Michael Nagin
Cover photography by Mark Mann

First Paperback Edition

146028962

To Jackie and Elena

D I S-CONTENTS

PREFACE

The longer I live, the more I'm convinced the world's just one big high school, with the cool kids always targeting the uncool.

—Me, *The Joy of Hate*, November 2012

Yes, I just quoted myself. Someone has to. But that quote also explains every thought I have about our existence on this silly orb called earth. The world is a high school, only more cruel, more reckless, and certainly more expensive. The lockers became apartments, the teachers our bosses, the guidance counselors our bartenders. Gym class has been replaced by health clubs, with Pilates now a substitute for climbing that horrible, horrible rope. The bathroom wall—a stinky billboard where grubby teens etched limericks and crude boobs—has morphed into the anonymous world of message boards, populated by cruder boobs.

Who runs the high school we all live in? The cool: people who consider themselves rebels and tastemakers for all that's edgy. They are now in control of defining the "conversation"—of deeming what is good and what is bad. Their power is drawn from their self-appointed cool—and a world that gladly forfeited character for an illusion of it. But it's all BS. In fact, if you scratch the surface of their cool veneer, you'll find that they're about as counterculture as a toupee, and not even remotely as useful.

My mission here is to provide the remedy to this vast world of pretension, envy, and hate, to write the guidebook on how to deal with the bullies and creeps who currently exercise free reign over us. This book contains a blueprint for those authentic Americans naturally inclined to rebel against the cool culture so lauded by pop culture, media, and academia. I speak of people I consider the Free Radicals—the true nonconformists who reject the lock-step cool that has become our society's most damaging fetish since autoerotic asphyxiation. Not that I've ever tried. I have an irrational fear of being discovered dead, contorted, and naked by concerned neighbors.

AN INTRODUCTION

Beliefs the cool use to enslave you:

- ► If you don't agree with them, no one will like you.
- ► If you don't follow them, you will miss out on something great.
- ► If you don't give in to them, you will die alone, and unwanted, possibly eaten by your army of starving cats.

Fifth grade was when life changed for me. It was during that sweaty, chaotic phase of life I realized there was something far more important going on in the world than saving to buy a speedometer for my Schwinn. It was a time of accidental boners, persistent pimples, and abject fear of, but endless curiosity about, the opposite sex. But it soon became something far more sinister.

It happened one morning, as class began in my suburban Catholic grade school in sunny San Mateo, California. A group of classmates showed up that day with a brand-new attitude and a mysterious excess of dangerous energy. It was as if they discovered a drug, one that tapped a keg of pure idiocy, disguised as higher consciousness.

Previously engaged and impressed by good humor, friendship, and grades, my classmates had changed, their demeanors replaced by something else. Something foreign. Something loud. Something stupid.

Apparently, the night before, they, like millions of impressionable kids around the country, had watched an episode of

1

Happy Days, the landmark sitcom about life in the late 1950s or early 1960s, when people still had parted hair and said things like "Sit on it" and "It's a war wound." This particular episode's plot involved gangs. I vaguely remember it, but I'm fairly certain Pinky Tuscadero makes a cameo, Potsie whines, and Ralph Malph cackles like a colicky, freckled rodent. There might have been a Hula-Hoop in the mix, and somebody somewhere in there got "frisky." I think it was Al.

After they watched the episode, it dawned on my classmates that creating a gang was the thing to do. This decision would instantly elevate them beyond the mundane sweetness of middle school, a time usually spent carving initials into desks and fighting spontaneous arousal with a double coat of underwear (a tip from the always helpful newspaper column Ask Beth). It turned them into rebels.

I think they called themselves the Sharks. And they spent that day, like "sharks," charging around the playground, running into other, smaller students, all while making idiotic wheezing noises they assumed sharks would make if they survived on oxygen. After instinctively dismissing this unruly new activity as silly and trying to organize some sort of alternative activity (nude four square), I became the target of their bullying. When I tried to reason with them—as much as a fifth-grader with acne can actually reason—I was banished.

And I've been there ever since.

This was my first encounter with the destructive superficial charms of cool: middle-schoolers who discovered a brand-new universe where achievement was not required to elevate esteem. This universe, it seemed, didn't value the actual success you might get from hard work. An animal name and a pack of friends gave these kids the sort of cachet they never had before. They adopted a new anti-life that had its own rules, and as silly as they were, it was just so much more interesting than everything that came before it. Plus, the girls thought it was neat. Suddenly all of the things that seemed pretty good before—companionship, Wacky Packs, exceptional schoolwork, nude four square—became "stupid."

It was now cool versus everything else that wasn't cool. The new world had begun, and I wasn't on the invite list. Fifth grade had just discovered the velvet rope. And it was held by lowbrow illiterates with snot on their sleeves. (Boogers were a major food group back then.)

From that first time that I found myself ostracized from the gang, I forever learned to beware of anything that smelled of manufactured, attention-seeking behavior. Everything from modern impractical fashion, to hip jargon that means nothing, to contemporary activism that helps no one but the activist sets off my anti-cool alarm.

For all cool was then and all it still is now is a different form of conformity. The more a group of people try to rebel, the more they are trying to fit in. And it is always at the expense of others. Cool is identified only by defining others as uncool. The velvet rope excludes before it invites.

Left and right. Good and evil. Republican, Democrat. Most people see the world split into two chunks. It's all we can handle. Two things. If you add a third, it gets weird. If you add a fourth, it becomes an orgy. And orgies are messy, from what Bob Beckel tells me.

In the last four years, these divisions have become more prevalent. Feminists versus religious institutions; black conservatives versus white liberals; gays versus churches (never the mosques); taxpayers versus redistributionists; public breast-feeders versus people who'd rather not see your breasts (unless there's a vacancy); clams versus oysters.

I believe this duality is unavoidable, but one division is wider and more pernicious. And it dwarfs the other divisions and wreaks more havoc than all of them combined.

That duopoly is the cool versus the uncool. And it's the cool-opoly, the monopoly of cool, that seeks domination. Pick a political, cultural, or moral universe, and in each one it's the cool who seek to punish, mock, or thwart the uncool. They do this freely and without much resistance, for exacting cool revenge is so common that the uncool let it happen without a fight—a sort of cultural Stockholm syndrome. Even as the cool put out ads condemning bullying, they spend the rest of their time turning persecution into an art form. The cool are just bullies with stylists and publicists.

From here on in, when I say "cool," I am referring to those people who, generally liberal, pretend that the predictable, acceptable choices they make are actual risks. They pat themselves on the back for making decisions that are cheered on by a media and pop culture who already agree with them. It's the engine driving so much pointless activism. The cool think, "If I embrace marching against war and capitalism, then I will be embraced by the famous people who also march against war and capitalism. Maybe I'll meet John Krasinski!" Their "rebellion" is a way to be liked and a way to be accepted by people they admire. And so the phony cool assume the mantle of edginess and contemporary cachet while mocking the dreary lives of the worker bee, the businessman, the religious family structure, the nonartistic clerk with a job he cannot brag about, the housewife, the occupant of a neighborhood considered drab, the man who enlists, the woman who rejects feminist fads, and me.

And if you're reading this book, most likely, you.

This bigotry toward the bland is neither harmless nor slight, but results in actual suffering, and even death. The desire to be cool overwhelms the most basic elements of logical thinking— sending morality from a vertical plane to horizontal. Instead of good triumphing over evil, they now exist side by side in a relativistic universe judged solely on the merits of being cool. In a world structured by phonies in Hollywood and elsewhere, good and evil take a backseat to Bonnie and Clyde. Being hip not only excuses the heinous—being heinous makes you hip. An ugly terrorist is a terrorist. A boyish one? Cool. Put him on the cover of *Rolling Stone*. He looks like a long-lost, slightly dazed Jonas Brother. He could be Jann Wenner's new intern. An intern with privileges.

We live in a time when a man who spent years as a prisoner of war after heroically defending his country is beaten handily in a presidential campaign by a young inexperienced senator who previously was known for organizing communities for purposes no one seems to remember. I mean, on the ladder of achievement, community organizing ranks slightly below selling celebrity toenails on eBay. But not anymore.

Was that simply an ideological and political battle, or was it something else? Perhaps Obama was a better candidate, but why, really? Only in the modern era can a bona fide war hero be depicted as a doddering old coot. And unless you're Keith Richards, you cannot be cool once you're over fifty-five. Once you qualify for the cover of the AARP magazine, you're toast. Might as well just get the Shirley Temple box set and a Hoveround. I have both, which is why the ladies love me.

In the McCain-Obama election, as in the one that followed, the variable that swayed the electorate was something new entirely. And that something new was the heightened culmination and demonstration of coolness. For many, voting for Obama was your entry to the cool club—a rejection of the same old faces and same old pasts. I mean, McCain probably didn't even have an Apple ID! It was better to elect someone whose face was not only new, but whose past was almost undefinable. Plus, he was young and black. I get it. If I were black, maybe I would have voted for him too. But I'd like to think qualifications also mattered.

In fact, in any place where something isn't cool, you will see these three words strung together: "old white men." Whether it's a clunky news editorial on gun control or a withering analysis of a Republican debate, the media will dismiss it with that handy cliché—they're just "old white men."

But the haters of the old white male forget that it was a hardy group of old white men who created this country . . . as well as a lot of amazing products that saved the lives of a whole bunch of other men (and women, black, white, and pastel). Sure, they were okay with a lot of other really crappy stuff (i.e., slavery), but compared with the rest of the awful, pitiless world, they were—literally—revolutionaries.

I have, throughout most of my life, veered toward the opposite of what's considered cool. A look at my yearbook photos reveals as much. My appearance veered between Greg Brady and a suburban Iggy Pop. When people had long hair, I preferred spiky. When crew cuts were in, I looked like Shaggy from *Scooby-Doo*. When kids embraced disco, I steered toward punk. And when punk became cool, I moved to metal. Now, as I am slightly older and a little less gorgeous, I listen to obscure, noisy electronica and doom metal that, at times, could clear the killing floor in a slaughterhouse. I enjoy stuff that accelerates my own exclusion. But it's not for effect. I do like the stuff. And I like being alone. (Which is lucky—the rest of humanity seems only too willing to oblige.)

My avoidance of mainstream entertainment isn't reactionary. I just tend to move away from stuff that bugs me and toward stuff that surprises me. It puts me on the outside of a lot of things, including the hip. It's how I became a conservative and, ultimately, a libertarian. My politics are simple: Leave me the hell alone, and take your definitions of cool and bullshit exclusionary language with you. My next step, I imagine, is to become a monk. (I actually am kind of serious. I toyed with making fruitcake, and own a number of hooded robes that I stole from hotels.)

Now in middle age, I've come to realize that avoiding cool will no longer suffice. For it has poisoned everything I know to be enjoyable and interesting in life. The concept of cool takes precedence over everything these days—from politics to personality, from food to fashion, from sex to safety, from climate to Colt 45s. Coolness is a replacement for a strong ego and operates as a safe, ambivalent response to evil in the world. The result: We are left with a dreary planet of self-esteem sponges more interested in capturing the approval of phonies than actually doing something real or positive with their lives. It's an attitudinal apocalypse. It's killing us, and we don't seem to mind.

The aftereffects of the cool revolution can be felt everywhere and are reflected in everyday behavior. We used to consider the right thing to do; now we consider the cool thing to do. In fact, the stuff we were once expected to take part in suddenly becomes cheesy, a waste of time. We've abandoned veterans' parades for divestment sit-ins and courtship for hanging out. Pop culture has replaced principle.

Instead of helping your parents through tough times, it's cooler to adopt a tiger through the World Wildlife Fund. Rather than quietly engage in traditions that keep a family together, it's just cooler to waste your money on a trip to Burning Man to find yourself. Rather than empathize with victims of terror, write a poem about the terrorist. Rather than visit an old folks' home, camp out in a city park and call the most liberating country in the universe a police state.

The end result? At the minimum, wasted lives. At the worst, death and destruction for the greatest nation ever. Cool is a path to nothing at all pleasing or constructive in the long term, a path that has paved over fine traditions—traditions that, in better times, were substantial activities that represented actual caring. When a teen decides to pierce his nipple, it's not just to make his nipple look like a different, cooler nipple. It's a middle finger to the people who loved and cared for him. He chose cool over them. I hope his nipple gets gangrene, falls off, and ends up in an omelet eaten by Liev Schreiber in an East Village diner.

Because, when it comes down to it, being cool means not caring. And not caring means inevitable decline. What cool does is tell people that decline is actually kind of awesome (if it's done with the right amount of ennui—see France), while acting mature and aging gracefully are quaint. And before you know it, you're that fifty-year-old idiot, sitting in the corner of a local bar, dressed like a Beastie Boy, your faded tattoos stretching over mottled fat like Satan's Saran Wrap, as you try to convince yourself that the worn-out chick with the gray Volvo eyed you up a second time. To actually give a damn about manners and elegance makes you a target of mockery.

The aim of being cool, really, is to say, "I am not like them. I am not a dork. I'm relevant."

Which is why everything done these days springs from a fear of dorkiness despite the fact that it's the uncool dorks who make the trains run on time. There's nothing more boring than a train schedule, but without it how would the hip find the right subway to that Williamsburg flea market where they can spend one hundred bucks on a T-shirt from a late-seventies Cheap Trick tour? (I was there—a stoner threw up on my shoes.) Without the uncool, the cool wouldn't exist. Why is that? Because cool contributes nothing to "how things work." Oh, something that appears cool can work (see everything made by Apple). But making such products does not rely on its makers being or appearing cool, but thinking and working hard. Behind that cool is a ton of very old-fashioned hard work performed by anonymous badasses. But they hide it—like the ugly coal plants that ultimately fuel every electric car.

The definition of cool: popularity without achievement. It's how President Obama got the youth vote. Ask any kid who voted for him, "Why did you do it?" and the convoluted, wide-eyed answer will ultimately translate into: "He's cool and that other guy wasn't." (Now they're paying the brunt of Obamacare. Suckers.) The media pushed this to the hilt, and much of the public bought it. Hope and change is cool because it sounds cool, even if it's undefined. An activist government is cool too, because giving stuff away is cool—especially when it's other people's stuff—and therefore perceived as philanthropic. But philanthropy without feeling the pain in your own wallet is super-easy to do, and about as cool as giving away your roommate's food while he's at work trying to pay for that food.

So what is perceived as cool in today's world, when it's really the opposite?

- **Bureaucrats spawned in teachers' lounges, chiseling away at your income through punitive taxation designed purely to redistribute wealth.** They care, you don't. You must be evil.
- **Dependency as an acceptable lifestyle, independent of achievement.** To the cool there is no shame in letting someone else pay your way, even if you could probably pay it yourself.

The government is your new boyfriend, with money (not his—mine and yours) and an apartment in DC. Embrace him. He absorbs the risk and distributes income so you can pursue whatever else strikes your fancy. In the old days feminists would mock women who depended so much on a man. Today if the man is the government, not so much. A man who opens the door for you is a Neanderthal; a bureaucrat who pays for your pills? A hero.

▸ **Ridiculing women, minorities, and gays who reject this culture of dependency and victimization.** They heroically say no to the worst kind of hood—victimhood. The lie here is that the cool defines itself as being outside the rigid structures of society, yet condemns those who really achieve that position in life. It's how Ben Carson can be roundly ridiculed, despite immense, earned success. And is there a truer rebel alive than Mia Love? Not to the media who ridiculed her.

▸ **Fake work that doesn't require building, moving, or doing things.** Anthony Weiner, a man whose only talent is aiming his camera at his dick, can embarrass himself and his family, yet happily return to run for elected office. He does so for two reasons: He doesn't believe he should have to actually "work" like the rest of us and he thinks the constituents agree. His return to the public eye (much like Eliot Spitzer and Mark Sanford) says a lot about a culture that has lost the ability to define real work. No wonder Mitt Romney was mocked as a superficial loser with no real accomplishments (as defined by the media). All he did was build a business empire and make money, for himself and others. And then, Christ almighty, he gave a ton of it away. Good riddance to the mean, old evil Mormon. Better to elect a guy like Obama, who spreads others' wealth around by force.

▶ **Movements that reject American values in favor of American guilt.** See Occupy Wall Street as one example, rejected by sensible Americans who dislike public defecation but coddled by the media, which ultimately left when the shit hit the fan, and street. How else can a Weather Underground terrorist end up teaching our kids on campuses instead of waiting for the needle on death row?

▶ **Anti-Americanism touted as appeasement to our international adversaries.** It's never "their" fault; it's always ours. Even when their brutality exists despite our benevolence (see the money we shovel into Egypt, as they continue to torture and kill Coptic Christians, a sect treated as an underclass by the Muslim Brotherhood). We used to advocate assimilation to recent immigrants; now we wonder if we haven't assimilated to *them* enough. The depth of this anti-exceptionalism is frightening. We have people flocking from horrible countries to ours with hopes of replicating here the same systems that destroyed their countries. It's happening in England, France, and now in Boston. Because of the cool view that America is fundamentally flawed, we cannot question those who come here to undermine the free-est, greatest country ever devised. *Maybe it is our fault for the Boston Marathon bombing*, ponder the progressive jackasses among us. And it allows for an insidious relativism, as witnessed in the comparisons of Muslim extremism to other kinds of religious extremism in the United States. But it's not apples to apples. It's apples to razor blades.

▶ **Evil in film as a lesson plan for a romantic, rebellious reality.** The cool's hold on society's throat is at its finest in the film industry. Any person, organization, or thing that rebels against structure is heroic, while anyone with a BlackBerry or

a briefcase is Hollywood shorthand for evil. He probably just
ate a baby. And not a free-range one, either.

▸ **If you question whether abortion should be seen as different from removing a tumor, then you must hate women.**
How can you deny happiness to everyone? (Fetus not included.) And that's why the cool—married to abortion at any
cost—seem reticent on the murderous abortion doctor Kermit
Gosnell. If he had used a gun, it would have been the subject
of an awful celebrity-laden music video.

▸ **Assorted slugs on death row are cool; their victims, forgotten roadkill.** This theme runs through art and pop culture like E. coli in a Tijuana cafeteria. There are more movies,
songs, plays, and websites about killers than about their victims. Victims are boring; their tormenters, deep. Hence there
are songs about Rubin "Hurricane" Carter and poems about
the Chechen bombers, but none about the folks they killed.
Disguised as empathy, this behavior is simply an exercise in
ego: The empathizer wants you to view them as cool for seeing beyond the obvious evil of the act. To the cool, empathy
is "deep." It's "challenging." To a tougher, more realistic past
America, it was "bullshit."

▸ **Politics is way cool, as long as it's progressive.** Conservatives by nature hate politics and politicians. Liberals love them
because it makes them feel cool. It's a must for everyone to
"be involved." Talk to any liberal friend and they're running
for office even when they're simply running their mouth. "I
have to tell you about the bake sale we had for homeless water
snakes." No you don't, but you will. Meanwhile, if you talk
about an issue that doesn't fit preapproved hip criteria, then
the "it's cool to be involved" premise goes out the window. Say
something about being pro-life, or pro-defense, or pro–death

penalty, and the crowd around you will fall silent. It's like admitting to cannibalism (unless the meal is a Republican).

- **Embracing amnesty and open borders.** Sure, other countries have borders (the ones most people are fleeing from), but discussing the possibility of an American border is smeared as racist—the ultimate in uncool. Am I a bigot for buying locks for my apartment door? No, but I'm probably racist for writing that. Amnesty is cool because it's so damn benevolent. "Hey you guys—why don't you just stay here, and not worry about citizenship!" Cool people love to make friends, and they will make eleven million of them. *Note:* To be cool, it's way cooler to have more brown friends than white. No one ever brings up amnesty when discussing immigrants from Eastern Europe or Ireland; they don't need more white friends. I wonder how the cool would feel if the new arrivals were looking to crash on their couch on the Lower East Side? As long as it's Arizona's problem, it's not theirs.

- **Anything old is uncool.** You can thank the media, of course, which seeks to portray anything traditional as dorky and outmoded. The stuff that worked before (in the good old days) apparently is stupid because it worked so well that it afforded us the luxury to trash it. It's great that Mommy and Daddy did all that uncool work, so you could sit in your air-conditioned classroom and shit all over them, to the approving eye of your ponytailed professor. He's just such a rebel. He writes letters to *Mother Jones*! (However, despite a distaste for tradition, the hip will pay thousands for a table made from salvaged, vintage "repurposed" snowshoes.)

- **Hero worship of celebrities based on fake edginess.** It pays to remind the worldwide media that Johnny Depp is not really a pirate, despite the jewelry and mascara he wears around the house. He's a walking thrift-store lamp. Doesn't anyone remember when he was just a twerp trashing hotel rooms? This worship of the play-actor further diminishes real work at the expense of the fake and affords a respectability to their political leanings that is wholly undeserved. Speaking of, I really hate . . .

▶ **Destruction masked as achievement.** Do moronic rock stars ever think of the maid when they trash their twenty-fifth hotel room? No rock video ever shows the poor minimum-wage worker (likely someone's mother) cleaning up that mess in slow motion; yet that's how all pop star destruction is depicted. As long as it's in slow motion, anything is cool. When Justin Bieber peed in that bucket and then swore at a picture of Bill Clinton as he exited a New York club, who did he apologize to? Not the poor cleaner who uses that bucket to mop floors. But to Clinton. Clinton's advice in response: Choose your friends wisely. (Spoken like a man with unsavory secrets.) It would have been nice if Bill said, "Treat people who aren't as lucky as you with respect," but then that would be against character. And would have creeped out the strippers.

▶ **Victimhood.** I often refer to the elevation of the David and Goliath myth as a universal storyboard dictating that it is always moral for the smaller party to win a battle over the bigger, even if that smaller and weaker party is evil. If America was a tooth, the cool would root for the cavity. A criminal is just a victim of your own success. And this must be rectified, by punishing you, either by taking your money through taxes or freeing the criminal so he can violate you one more time. Mumia Abu-Jamal—the cop-killing hero—must be innocent. He's got dreads! That's an even smaller minority than "black

males on death row." If he were also transgendered, he could
be the coolest person in America!

▸ **Code words.** Language that aptly describes things is uncool.
However, euphemisms created to avoid hurting the feelings
of our adversaries are not. Cool is removing judgment from
your lexicon. Hence, Fort Hood terror is "workplace violence."
Which I guess makes Hurricane Sandy a "weather tantrum."
Code words are now being employed to erase the meaning of
welfare, unemployment, loafing. Stress is now a word used to
describe everything that was previously known before as "life."
Saying "that's life" is uncool. Say "that's stress" and you're an
expert. Referring to someone who is in this country illegally as
an "illegal" is totally uncool—and on some campuses, "illegal"!
In the same vein, calling someone a "drug dealer" is bad too.
From now on they'll be known as "unlicensed pharmacists" or
"pharmaceutical entrepreneurs." Shoplifters are "nonspending
customers." Abortion is "women's health," and raising taxes is
"revenue growth." All of this is a clue: Because the cool cannot
call something what it is, they must resort to this Orwell-speak
to fool us into believing they're not morally bankrupt. When
you think about it, "cool" is just a cooler word for "liar."

▸ **Talking about your identity.** If someone cool happens also
to be gay, bisexual, transgendered, Raëlian, or Eskimo, you
and I will hear about it. If you are less proud of *what* you do
than *who* you do, then you're considered cool. We've moved
so far from a color-blind society that even the color-blind
have their own society. If you need to tell me you're gay, I'm
thinking you're not really gay. You're just boring. Right now,
as I write this, the media is reporting that a gay man is trying
to make the NFL as a field goal kicker. Remove "gay" from

the equation, and the reporter has to find another story. That story, however, will *never* be "Gay man doesn't give a shit about being gay."

Stretch this infestation of cool-aid over the past three decades, and it's no wonder the streets are flooded with asexual mopes who talk from the backs of their throats as they bowl in Brooklyn, ironically. How we got to a place where men in skinny jeans rank higher in achievement and status than men in military-issued camouflage is a mental journey beyond the limits of my simple, sodden brain. (Granted, it's a short journey.)

Why is this duopoly, the cool versus the uncool, so important? It won an election, among other things. Showbiz beat substance. Style creamed success. This happens in a culture that salivates over youth, glamour, and glibness. Fashion has no use for Mitts.

But the funny thing about cool? It's not cool. At all. In fact, what's truly cool is the rebellion against the perceived, predictable tyranny of cool. Conservatives, in my mind, should be cool. But they aren't. Some of it is their fault. You can't wear a blue blazer everywhere or carry a worn-out copy of *Atlas Shrugged* and not be immune to criticism. I've tried. They were brutal to me at the gym. But that's not all of it.

Why aren't conservatives cool? It's a fair question. From my experience being around conservatives, it's extremely frustrating how dismissive they are of "weird" things, and that hurts them. For example, I choose my music for my segments on *The Five*. My choices are never met with "That's good" or "That sucks." It's always rewarded with anguished looks on the other panelists' faces and the two-word review, "That's weird." Conservatives must understand that what is often perceived as weird becomes, later, something universal and accepted. (See *Cool Whip* and *Boxer Briefs*, separately.)

The truth is that conservatives do have the cool message. It's, "Step off." Or, for you old-schoolers, "Don't tread on me," which applies domestically and internationally. It's not cool to have a government intrude into every aspect of your life, under the guise of "help." The new electorate must learn this, or we are doomed. The so-called cool seems cool with drones (i.e., passive, antiseptic warfare). How uncool is that?

But we know there is nothing cool about dependency. There's nothing antiseptic about drones. And there's nothing cool about anti-exceptionalism, increased regulation, government control in all sectors, and a factional country based on race and gender. *We are the rebels.* What's cool is building businesses, military supremacy (which keeps us free to be cool), unity over division (once called patriotism), individualism, and competition (which is the universal engine for self-improvement). All of this may sound dorky, but it's as cool as Pegasus making out with a unicorn (i.e., very cool). We need to teach people how to love this country for the reasons that made this country what it is. And those reasons are so cool, it's no wonder Sean Penn, Michael Moore, and Robert Redford don't get it. They hate those reasons as much as they hate you for cherishing them.

It shouldn't be too hard, as an anti-cool campaigner, to win converts with a message like that. But we haven't. Which means this book must be a wake-up call for the rest of us, the uncool. It's time for the reign of the new cool. We have the message. We just need the messenger. He doesn't need a leather jacket. He just needs a thick skin.

Fact is, the desperate desire to be cool has skewed our culture toward nihilism, carelessness, and ineptitude. It is now cool to be an idiot. A jackass. It's cool to be a failure, as long as your failure is the basis for a reality show. And on the reality show you can do what's considered ultimately cool: "raise awareness." How else can you explain the Bravo network? It's a machine devoted entirely to the adult tantrum.

In the rest of this book, I will explore how cool has undermined all the best things about America. I will present a case as to why the desire to be hip is destroying the hippest thing we have: our ridiculously cool exceptionalism. I will reveal how the adolescent media and their infantile preoccupations are killing us, figuratively and literally. And then I will nominate the truly cool people on this planet who can defeat these hacks and phonies. They are the real matinee idols of this new movement—people I refer to as Free Radicals. There are more than you think. And far more than the cool want you to know.

UNCTUOUS OCCUPATIONS
AND POPULAR PURSUITS

You know what defined a cool job in the old days? I don't. I wasn't born yet. That's why it helps to read other people's books. In Joseph Heath and Andrew Potter's fantastic tome *The Rebel Sell*, they mention a study from the 1950s by Vance Packard, which teased out five factors that gave a job prestige. They were: importance of the task performed, the level of authority the job gives you, the know-how required in doing said job, the "dignity of the tasks required," and, of course, the money made from doing the work. According to Heath and Potter, the results—like my thigh rashes—were "remarkably consistent." Supreme Court justices were seen as the most prestigious, but also scoring high were exactly what you'd expect if you remember any black-and-white movies: bankers, executives, ministers, and professors. In those movies, they were usually played by Fred MacMurray or Robert Cummings. They had great hair and no visible tattoos. You know they smelled of cigarettes, Brylcreem, and work. They were rarely involved in "raising awareness."

How things have changed. With the exception of professors,

there's absolutely *nothing* still considered cool on that list. Ministers? They're the butt of jokes. Supreme Court justices? Please, the media even hates the black one (in fact, they *especially* hate the black one). Executives are just cogs in a machine, and as for bankers—even bankers hate bankers. My God, I'm a right-wing libertarian, and I hate my bank. Yes, as H and P point out, the prestige of all these jobs is "steadily waning," as the new, cooler occupations are picking up the slack. It's the "cool, bohemian creative types" that now get the chicks, and get movies made about them. Cinematic action is steadily being eliminated by slight men pressing "send."

It really is invigorating.

I'm not kidding. I was biting my nails during *The Social Network*, and I'm not even sure why. I mean, it was a movie about *rich kids suing over who invented a social networking site*. This was not *Dirty Harry*. Christ, it wasn't even *Hello, Larry*. It was *Goodfellas* for zeta males.

I don't begrudge the founders of Facebook. Anyone who creates something that millions—or billions—crave is genuinely cool in my book. It is why, however, I don't think Apple is cooler than McDonald's. Both make something that is a pure popular product. A Big Mac and an iPod are pretty much the same thing—except one has a slightly metallic aftertaste (I blame the lettuce).

But here's the catch. We live in a time when some products are cool while others aren't. And this cool bigotry masks a different kind of disdain—one directed at the nonintellectual, the guy who doesn't watch *Girls*, shop at Whole Foods, or read *Dwell* on the bidet. This average dude is not interested in the healing powers of crystals or windmills, or solar power. He's just fine with natural gas. His own, and North Dakota's.

This product bigotry creates the cool job elitism. Everyone wants to work for Twitter, but no one wants to work for Exxon. Try finding a job right now at Twitter. Impossible. But they're hiring in North Dakota. (Can a healthy unemployed individual fresh out of school frack? Or is that the modern equivalent of going to work for a fascist death squad—that eats kittens?)

Thanks to the rising cool status of certain jobs and the decline of others, people have stopped contemplating doing the dirty work, the work that keeps the lights on. Can you imagine a young college graduate announcing to his friends he is going to work for an oil company? Nope, he's joining an improv group instead. As I write this, the Labor Department reports that only 47 percent of Americans have a full-time job. That's because it's hard to get full-time work as a maker of artisanal tricycles. Or worse, edible artisanal tricycles.

In February 2013 it was revealed that Facebook paid no income taxes for 2012. As reported by CNN, among other places, the social network was due a tax refund of almost 430 million bucks. Now, this is a company that made one billion before taxes (which buys approximately 50 million hoodies for Mark Zuckerberg). But they were able to secure the refund because of a tax deduction from stock options issued to Facebook employees.

I won't pretend to understand how this works (as an English major, I have no discernible skills other than spelling *discernible* correctly), but I know this: that because this company happened to be Facebook, the story was a one-day affair. It came and went like an ice cream headache, leaving neither a bruise nor a hickey on the Zuckerberg Empire. If this company were something *that actually made something in a factory or field*, it would be roundly condemned by every single media hack on the planet.

Case in point, we have a strident administration that rails

against oil companies constantly (while taking credit for its record-breaking output), and the rich in general, over their perceived failure to pay their "fair share." Both entities are evil, for they make stuff people want, and because of this, they make a mountain of money. And from that mountain of money, the government takes a hefty slice. Which bureaucrats then spend on extremely important stuff—like a study into why lesbians tend to be overweight. (I could have answered that question: It's called pastry.) At one point, back in February, on Al Sharpton's show (I believe it's on MSNBC, a network for grad students suffering from shingles), President Obama made a petulant observation that what unites the Republican Party is protecting the rich from having their taxes raised. Well, then . . . what about your friends at Google, Twitter, and Facebook, Mr. President? Don't they have to pay their fair share? If Obama got any more adolescent, I'd have to ground him for a week and take away his Twitter privileges. No more selfies at memorial services for world leaders.

And so, fossil fuels, a boring, banal, greasy, dirty evil thing that is used by everyone (especially the poor, minorities, and women), are trashed daily by our commander in chief. Meanwhile a social networking tool—built by a social networking tool—that monopolizes the time of schoolgirls and the fat pervs who befriend them gets off scot-free.

Why is this important? Because one item produces energy while the other steals it. Without oil, we'd be nowhere. With Facebook, we are nowhere. Facebook has become the anti-oil, the anti-energy phantom that steals time and effort from everyone under the false pretense that you are actually *doing* something when you're only friending an ex or "liking" a picture of the ex's hideous children. And make no mistake, if those weren't your kids, you'd think they were ugly too. (This is based on my own research finding that everyone thinks their own children are 450 percent better-looking than they really are. This illusion of attractiveness was created by nature to keep parents from strangling offspring when the brats wake you up at 3:00 a.m. screaming like feces-spraying gremlins. I know, I'm sure that when I have kids I will think they are adorable too . . . before I leave them in the forest chained to a tree.)

We live in a time when the industry we need most is vilified and the one company that distracts us from reality gets a pass because it's coming from somewhere cool: Silicon Valley. A place where silicon people live.

Seriously, remember that old James Dean flick *Giant*? Guys working in oil fields, to me, seemed pretty damn cool. Now they're seen as the problem. Instead we look to pale, skinny men in hoodies and say, "Yes, that's cooler." I get the change in culture; I just don't have to like it. (Note: I own two hoodies.)

And where does that lead us? The vilification of the most uncool thing invented since Satan invented the Republican: fracking. By now, you probably know what it is. To put it simply (it's the only way I know how), it's a way to get natural gas and oil out of the ground by blasting shale (rock) with a method of hydraulic fracturing that is so far over my head, it might as well be happening on Neptune. But the real story is this: Certain parts of the United States that an observer might previously have described as "bleak" are experiencing a money-drenching boom so amazing that the only people who could despise it are environmentalists and the infantile celebrities who mimic them. Now we have intellectual giants like Yoko Ono and Rosario Dawson lecturing us on the dangers of fracking as if they've spent years studying oil and gas extraction. (At least I admit I'm coming at this issue armed with a limited knowledge of the exact science, but I've also read the studies and listened to both sides.) My guess is that neither of them or their like-minded dipsticks have a clue what a positive impact fracking has had on millions of Americans in an otherwise desperate, flat economy. My gut tells me, they don't care. It's not about being right, or admitting you were wrong. Let's be honest: The people fracking most benefits, Yoko and Rosie despise. Why isn't that a form of bigotry? They're "frackist," which is essentially hating the poor and uneducated—or, at least, those less rich and "enlightened" than you. Which essentially includes anyone between the coasts who doesn't meditate to the music of local Native American artists.

Why would some of these anti-frackers choose to repeat falsehoods about fracking (like saying it leads to breast cancer) when it's clear that they know little about the science? Because it's cool. And it's easy. You can do it while getting a back rub at the Virgin flight lounge.

The coolest kid in the anti-fracking movement is a guy named Josh Fox, who made a film called *Gasland*, a one-sided demagogic attack on fracking. It was later fact-checked by one of the real Free Radicals of our time, Phelim McAleer. McAleer is the guy who made the flick *FrackNation*, which counters the fearmongering of *Gasland*. But that's not what makes it great. What makes it great is how it was made: with a crowd-funded campaign that gathered over two thousand contributors to help pay for it. Those who donated were nobodies whose average offering to the film (according to my good friend Wikipedia) was sixty bucks. How is that not cool? Isn't that what a grassroots campaign is all about? If only the movie were about Noam Chomsky's fitness routine. Then George Clooney would've funded the whole thing himself—just to make sure his European neighbors would like him.

As I write this, experts are saying that fracking will now supply the United States with centuries of domestic energy, making it a possibility that in our lifetime we may free ourselves from a dependency on foreign nutjobs who take our money while funding terrorists who want to kill us (no, not the BBC). Yet we have a legion of cool-driven, egomaniacal freaks who'd rather have us under the thumb of the Saudis than reaping the benefits of homemade fuel.

Hell, if you'd rather not bomb Syria, and quietly excuse yourself from the riotous table that is the Middle East, isn't the only appropriate solution to get up, go home, and frack the hell out of each other? You don't even need a condom!

John Sexton at Breitbart.com covered a special version of hell: a "celebrity bus tour" organized by Josh Fox through the town of Dimock, Pennsylvania, to raise awareness on the evils of fracking, as part of the Artists Against Fracking campaign. Aboard the bus: Yoko, Sean Lennon, and—making this bus truly talent-free—Susan Sarandon (which sort of makes her the Ringo of this particular tour, but whatever). Their goal was to fight against fracking's "violence against nature," as Arun Gandhi, the grandson of Mahatma, explained. And he hoped to get the media to buy into their war against usefulness. Gandhi told the friendly *Huffington Post* that fracking would "destroy us, destroy humanity." This is the beauty of cool activism—no exaggeration is too overboard because outright lies and panic-stirring rhetoric only reflect the deep passion you have for the world. Did anyone mention to them that the bus they were on wasn't being fueled by windmills? These people are so stupid that if you told them the bus was powered by unicorn farts and Pegasus feces, they'd buy stock in it (God knows they're rich enough). When you lack truth, all that's left is exaggeration. And having Yoko's phone number on your cell? That's got to make them feel special. Look what she did for the Beatles.

Sexton explains that Artists Against Fracking (can we really call Sean Lennon an artist? What the hell has he painted lately? His toenails?) was created to lobby New York governor Andrew Cuomo to stop fracking in his state. They chose Dimock for their sorry publicity stunt because some families there had complained that their water was contaminated by fracking. Maybe it was. But, as Sexton points out, "The EPA tested wells in Dimock last year and in July issued a report stating that the water was safe to drink." This is Obama's EPA, mind you—an entity just left of the 1950s Politburo. But facts like that don't matter when you *feel*. And it's just not cool to change your mind—even if admitting you're wrong could possibly benefit an entire country.

While this tour got press, as did Matt Damon's miserable failure of another anti-fracking movie called *Promised Land*, something else didn't garner nearly as much attention—a leaked four-year study on the safety of fracking that made its way into the *New York Times*, and its blockbuster conclusion: Fracking is safe. It will not cause water contamination, which means Rosario will have to come up with some new claim—perhaps that fracking kills bullied, troubled teens by denying them the scenic awe of a local windmill?

Boring alert—here's a quote from the report, via the *Times*:

> By implementing the proposed mitigation measures the Department expects that human chemical exposures during normal HVHF [fracking] operations will be prevented or reduced below levels of significant health concern.

Man, is that boring. And when facts are boring, they're also uncool. Because you can't use mundane information to create a movement of angry people. You really can't get passionate over something so plain, so straightforward, and so damn factual. Matt Damon can't make a movie out of that. Well, unless he changes the actual facts. (And Saudi oil sheikhs wanted to fund it.) But Hollywood would never do that, would they? I trust Oliver Stone to keep it real.

Fact is, the only industries deemed cool these days are ones that generate disposable pop culture, whether it be music, films, designer jeans, indigenous peoples' jewelry, deejay booths for infants. Anything that actually helps you get to work on time cannot be championed without instantly becoming uncool. Perhaps this is because so many of these anti-fracking activists never have to go to work on time. Or go to work, period.

But there is an upside to our country's down market. When people need to watch their money, cool dies and the uncool comes to save the day, which is why I'm optimistic about fracking, and my home business, etching nudes of Lou Dobbs.

You know what I watch on TV? *Shark Tank*. You know why? Because it pits entrepreneurs against wealthy "sharks" in an effort to persuade the sharks to invest in the entrepreneurs' start-up projects. I enjoy it because products that are cool are shot down quickly, while other, boring ideas get cash behind them. Nobody invests *real* money in a loser project just because it's cool. In a recent episode, one of the sharks, Daymond John, told someone trying to sell him sunglasses made of wood that "all the cool brands are broke." The entrepreneur asking for money expressed reticence over entering general retail, of having his fledgling product end up in such horrible places like . . . God forbid, Costco. Yeah,

Costco—the modern capitalist equivalent of the pyramids, without the slave labor.

"Cool and profit are two different things," explained John. And it's something every young kid needs to hear. There's nothing wrong with making a profit by creating something that people actually need, even if it's as unglamorous as motor oil. Shit, if I were in my twenties, I'd head to North Dakota, frack the crap out of the place, and save my money for a neon robot dinosaur (it's been a dream of mine).

But once you start thinking about "cool," and letting it poison the well, you fail.

The guy making the glasses, as he pleaded for investment, said he would rather be in a boutique than a place where America actually shops. John responded, "Most people would say, 'I don't want to ever be in Walmart.' I'm dying to be in Walmart." And he rejected the guy. In my book, John was cool before he said that. He just became cooler.

There is nothing uncool about making something and selling it in places where people actually shop. We all can't be artists brunching in Soho, buying all of our goods at inflated prices from a chap named Sven in thigh-high leather boots, sporting a breast on his head. A truly cool person knows how superficial and fleeting cool really is. He finds something better to do with his time and his money. The great thing about America is that that person is usually rewarded for his hard work, which allows him to hire all of these other, miserable cool people to sell his merchandise. It might be the greatest reward of becoming successful, making an incompetent cool person work late.

THE PITIFUL PLOY
OF THE BAD BOY

For most of us, high school is the first site for the battle between good and evil. Between the stable and the shallow. Between cool and uncool.

I'm not a parent (unless you count the dolls I made from coconut and twine and named after members of One Direction), but I have often witnessed firsthand how cool operates on kids and forces them to do things that purposely mess with their internal instruction manual. Trying to be cool, as a goal, forces you to ignore any lessons ingrained by the people who made you. It takes a special, smart kid to resist and endure the torment that follows when you kick the cool to the curb.

The cool hate nothing more than when a genuinely original thinker rejects them. The cool need recruits to survive. Teens that reject them with a smile on their face destroy the most destructive movement in modern civilization. Rejecting cool, these brave kids help build the muscles of their ego and self-esteem that will be invaluable when they hit the real world. And when—inevitably—the real world hits them.

I have a friend who has two kids, both on the front lines of cool. One is seventeen, the other nineteen. Together that's thirty-six, or around the average age of a miserable divorcée.

Every day, teens weaker than these two succumb to the power of cool. They engage in behavior that they might otherwise find silly and destructive. Cool is a weapon created by creeps to obliterate the morals that good parents instill in their children.

My friend Tom and his wife have done a bang-up job raising their kids, but even I know that that isn't enough. Good parenting, from my perspective, is like building a three-foot retaining wall against a four-foot wave. The kids have to make up that extra foot. That wave wants to drag them into an undertow where sound judgment is suspended, where the valueless, uncaring, and ultimately nihilistic cool reigns. In other words, where the Kardashians are royalty.

I'm talking about prom night.

Back in April, I was out west, visiting my feisty mother. (She's eighty-eight and ornery.) Sitting in our backyard, Tom's daughter, a senior in high school, was asked by her mom about the prom. "I'm not going," she responded, without any emotion. This came to her dad and mom as a shock, but the daughter, Mary, could have been describing a lost scrunchie. She'd already moved on. Because she's smart.

But wait: She had a cute boyfriend! She had picked out a dress! She was going to get her nails done! (All twenty-two!) Her mother asks her about her boyfriend, and she says, "He's not my boyfriend anymore." Then she started texting (a habit that has now replaced breathing for anyone under twenty-five).

We didn't press her for details, but I realized that I was witnessing a banal routine that plays out every year around the prom. It goes like this:

- Girl gets asked to prom by guy, who may or may not be her boyfriend at the time. He's probably a year or two older. If the gap is wider, look into it: He may be her teacher.
- Boy sees prom as a "milestone"—an opportunity to take whatever you call a high school relationship to the next level. I remember this well, even at forty-eight years old. The prom was all about getting booze and a hotel room off the highway and getting lucky. It's weird to observe this play out with your friend's kid. You want her to do the right thing, even if thirty years ago you were rooting for the wrong thing.
- The girl is forced to make a choice: go along with his plan, or else lose out on this special night and spend that evening surfing the Web for cat videos, listening to Justin Bieber, and eating Häagen-Dazs in her jammies. (Which I recommend, by the way—always relaxes me after doing *O'Reilly*).

Boy applies pressure to girl as the prom approaches. The big day is the big payoff for her—and the boy knows this. She's been thinking about this since she was in junior high. I know I was. I even made my own dress (out of Fruit Roll-Ups).

Of course, you don't want to mess up your opportunity to go to the prom, the dude will tell her. He dangles that evening in front of her like a cool carrot thereby getting her to give in to his demands that she drink, do drugs, and whatever else. If she refuses? Then, maybe, he'll say aloud: The prom isn't really a good idea after all. And perhaps there are other girls who would really enjoy his company. (He mentions, jokingly, *those are girls who will do things*.)

Thankfully, for this particular girl, this time-tested game plan backfired, and she said, "Get lost," to the creep. She ended up going to the prom on her own. (I'd go with her, but there's an age cap at twenty-one and it would be really awkward considering the outstanding warrant.)

As for the boy, he gets to live with the fact that he blew it. He may never figure that out, but who cares? Maybe he'll learn that the girl who says no is the girl you want. But if he doesn't, that's his loss. And every good girl's gain.

And this good girl resisted the first sinister strategy of the cool, which is to denigrate you if you refuse to be cool. And then punish you when they find out their cool cunning did not work. The cool must crush your spirit, because you've marginalized theirs.

If this were a video game called "Don't screw up your life," this girl successfully navigated the first level. If you want to see how the failures end up, look up any ex-girlfriend of a major rock singer. They now look like Willem Dafoe, on a good day. You avoid that reality by not making a habit of saying yes to bad ideas just because they are cool. And to bad boys. Who are generally just losers.

But perhaps unconscious of a greater achievement, she rejected the primary engine of cool that leads many young girls to ruin: a desire for acceptance.

Here's the sales pitch honed among horny high school boys: "What if the world would end tomorrow?" "Would your self-restraint have made you any happier when you're dead?" "It's just uncool to wait—what with a meteor on its way." "I'm leaving for college, and things are different there, you know?"

This line of reasoning, really, only works on stupid women. But there are millions of stupid women out there—almost as many as stupid men. But stupid women let stupid men sleep with them, which accounts for so many Maroon 5 fans.

Falling for this cool move can actually alter the course of your life, forever. And not for the better, unless "for the better" means "living above a laundromat in a forgettable town, putting your-self to sleep with *Grey's Anatomy* reruns and prescription cough syrup." (That describes two years of my life—and they weren't the worst years.)

But, still, cool kids try to make this big lie stick. Their strat-egy: convince you that if you don't hang with the cool kids, and do what the cool kids do, then you will never be cool.

If you need evidence, go to any city run by a liberal mayor and look around. It's full of people who said yes, to anything and everything. Pensions, programs, boondoggles—all costing billions—to feed the egos and the pockets of the powerful and corrupt. Oakland, Chicago, Detroit, DC, Smurf Village—these are cities built on "yes." Which is why they have nothing left but one big "NO." And that "no" is the answer to the question, "Should I think of moving there?"

God, what I would give for a society to relearn the pleasures of saying no. Not just to premature sex and smoking dope and wearing saggy pants, but *to everything.* My gut tells me that the countries that will own our asses in the next century are those who say no, calmly and regularly (e.g., China and Gabon). If I had my druthers, I'd create a robot that simply says "NO," and run it for president. There is nothing in the Constitution that says you can't have a robot as president. If that were the case, we'd never have elected Calvin Coolidge (the greatest robot president we've ever had).

The point of cool is to erase your ability to say no. Saying yes buys you cool cachet, but it always ruins your life later. And it does, trust me. There are things I said yes to when I was younger that I regret. That stint stripping in Prague did me no favors. There are old men with photos.

And of course, cocaine. (Let me save you time if you're

contemplating that experience: Drink thirty cups of coffee and find someone else who has done the same, and start talking inanely. It's sort of like how Jim Carrey is without drugs. If "cool" has a mascot, it'd be an eight ball.)

The best way a young girl can respond to the aggressive pressure of boys during this period of her life is to say this: "Your intense desire to have me is proof to me that there will be many, many more boys just like you who want my company. I thank you for that information, but I'm going to wait for the next bus to come along. Whatever is on it will be better than you. And I'm including the homeless guy without pants." By saying no, she wins.

Mind you, it's not the boys' fault. During that age, they are senseless beasts, ruled by their precocious, mindless weenies. But it's the deal their stupid weenies make with their brains that gave birth to cool. This is my theory, anyway. There is no other reason for popping your collar or wearing sunglasses at night or wasting hours in the gym staring at your abs. Cool was created to subject the most mediocre of minds to the most tedious of penises. You want proof? Jon Bon Jovi. Is there a more tedious penis that ever lived? Imagine getting up every morning, asking yourself: "What clothing would a man half my age wear? And why am I slowly turning into Jane Fonda?"

'Tis true: The reason for "cool" is to feed that organ primarily responsible for planet earth. Think about it. If we were governed solely by our brains, we'd never actually procreate. Who in their right mind would want to create the screaming, pooping mess we have come to call an "infant"? If it weren't for the urge for sex, who would actually agree to such a horrible deal? Imagine there is no sex, and it really is a stork who arrives and says, "Here's a thing you have to take care of for twenty years, and it will hate you for fifteen years of it." No thanks, says the brain.

That's why the penis created cool—to get women past their common sense, the incredible fortress of reason called the brain. Women didn't invent cool, they didn't have to. They were born cool. They don't need men; they just need dolls and Easy-Bake Ovens. And later *Project Runway*, capri pants, and overpriced sushi. Cool is an evolutionary tool to unzip women's jeans and to further men's genes.

Of course, the cool kids have no idea that what they're engaging in is really just another biological trick. They actually think they're being cool, and being rewarded for it, when in fact they're just mindless fleshy masses attached to a throbbing node, which is making all their dumb decisions for them. Acting cool is actually just well-worn circuitry employed by millions of men since the beginning of time. If cavemen could have formed rock bands and invented leather jackets, they would have. But they were too stupid and dying at nineteen. Like many rockers do.

Initially cool was a disguise by the weaker male to get good girls to mate with weak or inferior men. Then cool, destructive behaviors like drug use, "not caring," or "hanging out" became mistaken for actual talent or character. Thanks to pop culture, which celebrates "dangerous" behavior in music and movies, the cool have reached a measure of stardom usually relegated to actual achievers. Hence acting. The whole point of being a movie star is to extend the cool prestige of high school to your entire life. And to bang girls who, when you're fifty, are pretty much still in high school (a shout-out to Woody Allen).

But for the rest of us, cool has a shelf life. If you're a quarterback in high school, you're cool. But ten years later, working as a sullen bouncer at the only nightclub in town, your "cool" is on life support. Which is why so many young girls who never said no end up with losers in pants hanging below their asses and no known income to speak of. These cads were charming in high school; now they're as useless as shoulder pads on a snake.

In the end, the winner is the female who says, "I can do better." The winner has an ego so strong that when the cool try to storm the gates, they drown in a moat of stoicism. While watching some murder trial unfold on Headline News, I asked my wife a simple question. "Would you leave me if you found out that I had killed someone?" I expected her to say, "I would stand by you." But without pause, she said, "I'd leave you." Of course, she often says this. But nonetheless, that's the kind of chick you want. She has no time for mystery, danger, or the trappings of a bad boy. To her, it's just baggage. And it should be, for all girls. And for all women.

This is not an epiphany. Any old lady born in the 1940s could tell you this. But cool redefined the positive attributes of your average male. A nonproductive commitment-phobic creep now becomes hip and mysteriously remote. The cities are full of women falling for the cool loser: the man trafficking in "edgy" so women cut him slack in his more loathsome behaviors. Christ, I know so many, it's sad. Please accept my flaws (and pay my rent) because I can play guitar! Badly.

Date an artistic male with issues, and chances are you begin convincing yourself that "this is what I get for becoming involved with a creative mind. This is the trade-off." But for the guy, being edgy and cool is just another way to have their cake and eat it too. Cheating, drinking, drugging—it's stuff accountants can't get away with but rock stars can. I am a writer, TV shouter, and author, but I married a woman who sees none of that. She only sees my behavior. (Which is my tough luck.) And when my behavior is lackluster, I am treated no differently from a man who sells Kenmore washers and dryers. If I get cocky, I get the couch.

Which is why I monitor my behavior. I don't have an ego. I have a built-in parole officer.

As my friend's seventeen-year-old daughter demonstrates, learning this lesson requires no age-ripened wisdom. It just takes a moral spine. It's the ability to get up and walk out, slamming the door permanently, when the cool desperately attempts to override your common sense.

Imagine if all girls called a moratorium on cool. How amazing would it be for women to stop demeaning themselves with morose jerks and actually demand decent guys. Maybe the best tip is this: Treat every day as though you're preparing for the prom. If it doesn't meet your expectations, make other plans. I'm free most weekends.

THE DEEP CREEP

B esides buying this book, what makes a person truly cool? A few decades ago, it might have been a leather jacket, a cigarette, some military service, a motorbike, and a bicep with an anchor tattoo. Perhaps a nickname like "Snake." But that's all changed. The dark and dangerous has been replaced by the earnest and annoying.

Probably in an effort to be cool and meet chicks in bars, two researchers decided to undertake a study to figure out what makes someone cool—now. Ilan Dar-Nimrod (I swear, that's his name), a postdoctoral social psychology researcher at the University of Rochester Medical Center in New York, and Ian Hansen (I swear, that's his name), an assistant professor of psychology at York College, decided to survey over 350 college students, asking them to name terms that described their perceptions of cool. They were then asked to rank how desirable these qualities might be in someone. (This would have been more fun if they were all naked, but that's why I'm not a professor.)

First of all, I have a problem with the group under scrutiny. If you really want to know what makes something or someone truly cool, the last thing you should do is ask a college kid. Ramen noodles? They're experts. Anything else? Zilch.

Whatever college kids find cool has trickled down from somewhere else. Usually a professor, a pop singer, or a drug dealer named Magic Carl. They tend to accept their mentor's idea of cool, without much thought. How else can you explain the popularity of poorly shot foreign movies, pointless causes, action figure collectibles, solemn but incoherent Asian tattoos, and unreadable books by Howard Zinn?

Anyway, I'd redo the whole study and ask people in their eighties. Or hell, nineties. You ask them what's cool, and they'll answer plainly: "Killing the Nazis." And they'd be right. It beats, "Getting signatures to support the rain forest."

Dr. Dar-Nimrod and Mr. Hansen's amazing work (which will be the name of the movie), published in the *Journal of Individual Differences* (you can find it behind *Cosmopolitan* at the supermarket checkout), included something Dar-Nimrod calls "cachet cool"—the steps required to create a really cool dude or dudette. Some of the findings were obvious: stuff like friendliness, competence, attractiveness (called the Gutfeld Variable) were seen as cool traits. Yes, this is about as surprising as girls hating spiders: We love hot, nice people. Especially if they smell good and actually talk to you while you perform your rigorous research. (It's the first time the author of the study talked to a girl in months!)

The cool attribute that strikes me as most important, however, is "social consciousness." According to the researchers, you are cool if you volunteer for socially responsible activities, which can mean anything from recycling crap to gathering signatures for something earnest (saving whales, slugs, or CNN's ratings). As someone who gathered signatures for the Nuclear Freeze maybe three decades ago, I get what this is about. People think you're deep and it opens doors. But it's 100 percent bullpoop. Because it's just too easy. Far easier than saying, "I fought for my country," which, apparently, isn't deep at all, despite the limbs lost.

Dar-Nimrod explains that these traits are more dominant than the clichéd cool of yore: The guy in sunglasses who smokes cigarettes is no more. Being "pro-social" is now replacing "risky behavior" in the realm of cool. Thrill seeking is now trumped by "feel seeking." (I invented that term just now—further proof that wine from a screw-top bottle helps my writing.) Forget Lee Marvin; it's now a callow lad in a PETA shirt who makes impressionable women swoon. That said: I wonder if the fact that a guy named "Nimrod" was doing research could really explain these findings?

Either way, I'm of the belief that pro-social behavior is just as deadly as smoking a Lucky Strike while pulling a wheelie on a Harley over a pile of undetonated land mines.

First off, let's strip away the illusion of what "social consciousness" really means. It's a euphemism for "liberal." When they're talking about social causes, you know they aren't referring to pro-life marches or NRA picnics. It's about gathering support for stuff like Greenpeace or Planned Parenthood. In our contemporary culture, caring about the unborn is about as uncool as soiling yourself in church. (I mean, seriously, what are you doing in church?)

On *The Five* I brought this up in a short monologue, pointing out the major flaw of these cool conclusions. Coolness—real coolness—is based on the prioritization of caring. Let me paraphrase myself, from whenever I said it: "The truly cool person reserves effort for people closest to them. In turn, they leave everyone else alone, until they have the extra resources to help them. They don't tell you what soda size to drink or how much to recycle. Social consciousness gets in everyone's business, while their private lives go to hell." And how that became cool is beyond my comprehension. Remember Gladys Kravitz? The neighbor from *Bewitched*, who was always in Samantha and Darrin's business? In the seventies that was annoying; in 2013, it's lauded. She's "engaged," she's "caring," she's also, in any era, a total pain in the ass.

Examples of this type of "Ignore Locally, Annoy Globally" abound, from saps like Jim Carrey to sappier saps like Sean Penn. You know their families dread their presence around the holidays because these thoughtful souls care more about gun control than about self-control. I don't know this for a fact—about those chaps in particular—but I know it from college years at Berkeley. The more people care about something far, far away, the less they care about their immediate surroundings—or the people they annoy within those surroundings. It's always the roommate who's obsessed with saving the orangutans whose personal hygiene is similar to one.

It's this kind of cool that harms more people in this world than the risky jerks who race through city avenues, high on stimulants, head to toe in red and black leather. Over the long term, symbolic attempts at appearing cool end up replacing honest charity that actually helps people. In most cases, social consciousness, really, is a simplistic strategy to mask a lazy intellect and fulfill a desperate need for attention. It's what liberals do when they don't get talk shows or are in a holding pattern waiting for talk shows. (See *Weiner, Anthony*.)

And it puts those who disagree with their antics at a disadvantage. How can you be against helping the poor? Or separating glass bottles from paper trash? How can you not want to save the whales, or adopt a polar bear, or marry a Baldwin?

You must be a monster if you don't agree with those causes. And while some of these activities might have some good effects, the persons engaging in such "selfless work" are really doing it for themselves. It's all about feeding an ego, not feeding a person. As I write this, Ben Affleck is going to live on $1.50 a day to raise awareness of the plight of the starving in Africa. Wouldn't it be better if he raised awareness as to why so much money raised for Africa rarely makes it to its poor, suffering people? Of course, it would—but that's not a stunt. That requires real homework, real research, and real knowledge about the nature of Third World corruption and its consequences. And Affleck has enough trouble trying to convince people he's not a hologram.

Social consciousness has become a gimmick to excuse reprehensible behavior. In fact, put "social" before any word, and it becomes "important" and "compassionate." At its worst, social consciousness masks evil—it's flimflam for the foul, a condemnation condom. Social consciousness won Al Sharpton invites to the White House, despite the cad's ruining countless lives since his garish orgy of racial exploitation that began with the Tawana Brawley case in 1987.

How do you know that social consciousness is thoroughly worthless? When it's so easy that everyone else is doing it. When it's integrated into sappy TV sitcoms, and when corporations desperate for approval from people who hate them flaunt it on their websites or on Twitter. When superficial and dumb-as-dirt celebs get involved. Social consciousness becomes the dumping ground for reflexive, attention-seeking acts of meaningless symbolism—a phony exercise meant to shroud the shallowness of those employing it. It's a sham's best friend. It makes you miss the cool of old: the aimless biker with a nonfilter cig hanging from his lips. Yeah, he smelled bad. But at least he won't block your path to work to get you to sign a petition to save the paramecium. And, for the record, paramecia are assholes.

On the ladder of cool, however, social consciousness maintains the top spot. At the bottom, hanging on to the lowest rung of uncool, resides its opposite: the boring capitalist. Meaning, the person who is greedy and always out for himself. The person making a buck is inferior to the person who gives a fuck. Never mind that the greedy dude is usually making a buck to support a family, and often a community. And, oh yeah, a country.

Of course, it's the boring capitalist who often bankrolls the people who hate him. If it weren't for the person bringing in the money, nothing else would work. For a community to grow to a size that sustains those who don't contribute to the growth of said community (whom I call leeches but society has chosen to call grad students), you need an immensely powerful creature to build a structure that allows those loafers to exist. But even a whale can only support so many parasites.

Without a "capitalist consciousness," there is no "social consciousness." A poor society cannot help the poor. This is why no one should listen to Al Sharpton. If it weren't for people Al Sharpton hates, there would be no Sharptons. This is troubling to me. Why is the average businessman boring but the radical type deemed cool? I came up with some possibilities:

- ▸ **Businessmen are boring on purpose.** The suit and tie and drab hair are meant to hide the inherent riskiness of capitalism. That's the irony: The real daredevils are those who play with their own money. Those who start businesses, who risk it all, and often who lose it all, over and over. Someone has to provide the funds for the safety nets the cool demand—and the providers are the uncool capitalists who took risks with their capital and are now taxed to the hilt. The vast majority of people supporting our national dependency are businessmen—large and small, male and female—who put their asses on the line every damn day. They are the truly cool, even if they look like dorks drinking Scotch and doing karaoke poorly in a Midtown bar (it's always to Taylor Dayne). The real risk-takers build products and then brands, while those railing against them are as safe as soy milk.

▸ **It's easier to understand caring than it is to understand business.** Ask any television news producer what makes more immediate, arresting television: a young, earnest protester railing against corporations, or a corporate employee defending his company? Perhaps if the producer took a course in "how money works," he might see the merits in the latter. But he didn't get into journalism to do math. He got into journalism to tell a story. (And generally, to speak truth to power, which really translates as "The speaker is a dick.") In that story, it's the emotional subject that trumps the uncool reality of life. Plus, you might score with the protester, who wants to get famous and get access to your minibar. The participants satisfy each other's needs while obliterating any sense of truth.

▸ **Business is anti-charismatic.** Banks are meant to be dull. There should be no flash accompanying your cash. Which is why we don't want Mickey Rourke to be our financial adviser; he'd put all our money in Eastern European brothels and expensive tequila that plays Pac-Man with your liver. We just want to drink with him. So attributes like "charm" and "sexiness" and "romance" never evolved in the business world. Meanwhile, the young men who lack the cash to get girls into bed have instead built an arsenal of anti-authoritarian lies to get laid. (I did this for a while myself, but it didn't work. I just can't grow dreadlocks.) How else could a piece of trash like Bill Ayers get laid? As a terrorist, this loser couldn't even do that right.

▸ **Guilt for being successful.** Once you're successful, there are others who are envious of your achievements, who blame you for their lack of accomplishment. (I've been on both sides of this, often on the same night.) Sadly, it works. Most of us are decent people, and we want to be liked and/or left alone. So when the cool anticapitalists—feeling no guilt because they've apparently never made a profit anywhere—choose to focus their "for the greater good" mentality on the benign capitalist, the benign capitalist capitulates. When these people claim that others "deserve" your income, your savings, your material goods, rather than fight the arguments, corporations and their captains give in; it's just better to throw money at angry fools than to argue with them. You can't win when you're a suit, and they are hirsute. Seriously—since when did lumberjack beards reflect actual achievement . . . on Brooklyn waiters?

▸ **Young people don't know where money comes from.** To them, it comes from Dad's bank account. Press them further, and you might as well ask them how to build a Hadron Collider. Sadly, no one bothers to educate the cool kids about money. Have you ever read an article about a penniless rocker who calls his mom to borrow cash so he can put money in his van's gas tank? No, you just read about his "dark soul." For some reason, the "cool" exist without the machinations of money; stuff just appears when they need it, like Easter eggs in April or Democratic voters in Ohio. It's far easier for them to understand "divestment on campus" than "investment in stocks." This is why students are often the best targets for the aggressive beggar. I see it in Manhattan every day. A seasoned panhandler need only play cool, and by proxy can make the backpacked undergrad feel cool too, and that quickly separates the kid from his dad's dollars. The panhandler walks away with money for dope, and the young dope walks away feeling good about himself, without ever wondering how that money made it into his pocket in the first place. That's the essence of modern capitalism for the cool: "I give you something, yet I have no idea where that something came from." It's an economy based on the tooth fairy.

It's this misguided view of charity that has replaced real charity. As our government pretends to offer handouts, it's really just spreading the wealth around, without wondering where that wealth has come from. In the end, redistribution kills ambition, saps the energy that fuels the American dream, and makes all of us poorer each passing day. Our consciousness may be raised, but our options for wealth and success dwindle. (Which is why I really need you to buy two copies of this book. My hormone treatments aren't covered by Obamacare.)

YOU PRAY, THEY DECAY

L et me ask you this: If you were to designate who was cooler, who would it be? Phil Lynott or Mitt Romney? It's pretty easy. Lynott—hands down.

Lynott was the lead singer who fronted the great Irish band Thin Lizzy, known for chord-crunching nuggets like "The Boys Are Back in Town" and "Jailbreak." If you don't have their great live album, you're probably an awful person. Anyway, Lynott died of a drug overdose in January 1986. He was a great-looking, talented, black Irish—but also a junkie. A dead junkie, now.

Back in September 2012, a couple of months before the last presidential election, both Lynott's widow and mom raised objections to Romney's use of "The Boys Are Back in Town" during his campaign. They were opposed because Mitt opposed gay marriage, and they assumed Philip would have been pissed about it, if he hadn't overdosed twenty-five years prior.

They have every right to object. If it were me, and my music were being used during the campaign of someone I disagreed with, I'd say something too. The only candidate I'd allow to play my music would be Bigfoot and, unless we're talking about foraging for squirrels, he's notoriously apolitical.

But viewed through the prism of cool versus uncool, another layer to the story begins to appear. A rocker's family objects to an uncool politician, one demeaned by our media to be a religious freak (because just being religious makes you a freak). Who wouldn't agree with the family? Me? I think it's cooler to live a semi-healthy life, one long enough to provide goods and services to the loved ones around you. That's cooler than dying from an overdose, whether you're gay, straight, or whatever Andy Dick is.

And so I offer one objection. The fact is the Romney family would have gotten way more love from our shallow society if they were champions of a liberal, ephemeral social consciousness instead of real, actual charity.

My friend Walter Kirn, a tremendous writer, and also a Mormon, will help me explain what most people don't know about that dorky, uncool religion. "Mormonism is the greatest example I know of an organization whose charitable work is neither denigrating to the recipient nor unduly guilt-inducing for the giver." He cites an example that I never heard of, because the media ignores it: Deseret Industries, a division of welfare services of the Mormon Church. "Deseret Industries is a kind of in-house Goodwill store–network that performs all the functions of Goodwill— job training, low-cost used goods—with none of the fanfare." (I know—imagine that—an honest-to-God charity the networks never bothered to trumpet. If Mitt were a liberal, and the charity focused on sex workers with webbed feet, we'd be organizing Live Aid II).

That's the key. Real charity has no fanfare. Social consciousness, however, is often nothing but that. It's fanfare designed to create fans for those publicly displaying their concern. Says Kirn of the side of Mormonism none of us heard about because no one in the media wanted to: "Combined with various schemes that can and do distribute foodstuffs and other household staples, the church offers members a comprehensive in-house welfare system that is underwritten by the ten percent tithing done by all faithful members." Ten percent—on *top* of what Mormons pay in normal taxes. Those evil, greedy religious nuts strike again!

I can't think of a more uncool word than "tithing." It's like the opposite of "social consciousness." But, in reality, why isn't tithing cool? John Lennon did it. It's charity, pure and simple. And it's charity that works.

And let's remember how this tithing is possible. Someone has to *make* money to make money for tithing available. Yep, it's the boring businessmen like Mitt Romney who supply the green to make that real, comprehensive charity possible. "This tithing obligation," says Kirn, "also supports a global missionary program, a worldwide temple-building program. Talk about efficiency. And the wonder of it is that by pooling their resources and doing so cheerfully and voluntarily, church members receive a sense of security, pride, and usefulness that causes them to give even more for specific projects as they come up." Amazing, right? This is how government is supposed to work. Instead, we get Obama phones, ACORN, and California.

Talk about uncool. Far better for those who ridicule people like Romney to embrace superficial "caring" than to admit that good men in suits with boring personalities are better at it than you. Better not to know the facts beyond the frosting. Fake caring is that frosting—no cake, just a sweet momentary sugar rush that makes you feel good without accomplishing anything but an ego thrill. It's way more exciting than tithing, so why bother with the real thing?

I bother, because we're now watching a false morality replacing a real one. I'm not a religious person. I'm half atheist, half agnostic (and all sexy). Meaning, in the daytime, I don't believe in God. But at night, alone with my thoughts, facing that gaping, terrifying maw without a rail to hold on to, I drift toward something less certain than nothing. Especially in a contract year.

My point: As nonreligious as I may seem, even I know that as our culture wanders further from a desire for universal truth, we find ourselves slogging through an amoral outhouse, following false gods because we've mistaken their cool for character. So, by all means, laugh at the uncool who make things work, and champion those who traffic in self-absorption masked as selflessness. It might make you cooler, but it won't make the world better. And if there's anything we've learned, you can't get any more uncool than God. In the high school that is America, God is, like, such a nerd.

What a silly, uncool idea that is. I get atheism. But that's not what gets me. There are plenty of atheists who find better uses of their time than denigrating the religious. My targets are those who trash religion to elevate their coolness. For them, bragging that they're a "lapsed Catholic" in order to nervously score cool points in a public setting just shows me how desperate they are for approval. (I've witnessed this more times than I can remember—i.e., at least three times.) The only thing you're "lapsed" in is your ability to discern a level of interest in your stupid, predictable asides about how dumb your religious family is. You've "lapsed" in an ability to put your family before feeling cool.

Fact is, the cool, who are almost entirely liberal by default, are also antireligious to a fault. You cannot be religious and cool. According to the purveyors of cool, God cannot be cool because He replaces badass, existential, beret-wearing, clove-smoking nihilism. And religion competes with the artificial charity of government, which exists to support you in your existentialism. And so liberals, by intent or by accident, have replaced God with government. President Obama is now their supernatural being—a spiritual leader who can do better than simply turn water into wine. He can make trillions of dollars disappear. Then, with a wave of his hand, he can just print more money! The loaves and fishes were amateur hour by comparison.

But you know what else is uncool about church? It's boring. It's repetitive. It's solemn. It's like a Charlie Rose interview. I hate it. Even more, no matter what charitable efforts you perform, if you're part of a real church, you can never brag about it (against my nature). There are no special buttons or ribbons. On the other hand, if charity is done as a stand-alone, detached from religion, that's cool. You always brag about it. I'm beginning to think cool has become a religion for those who find the organized practice so difficult to absorb. I don't blame them: Religion runs counter to my own internal logic. But my skepticism does not cloud my analysis that going to church might be something slightly more positive than ridiculing those who do. God may not exist, but at least I realize that those who believe in Him (or Her) are often nicer than the people who seek approval through ridicule of faith. It's no longer about believing in God or not—it's about having people kneel before you. You're the false god, and your only commandment is that people like you. And, possibly, find it kind of sexy too, ya know?

TREATING CRAZIES
LIKE DAISIES

I know crazy people. I grew up in California. I've seen them up close. And it's never romantic; it's never pretty; it's just scary. I once had a girlfriend who worked at Napa State Hospital (or was a patient there—it's all pretty hazy), the asylum where the Cramps once played. (Look it up—it's pretty wonderful.) The way she described it was about as romantic as an ice-cold bedpan, which was how she described our relationship, alas. Back on topic, from afar, the insane are often idealized to a point of sacrificing one's own safety. "Wow, they are such kooky fun." But would you let one cook for you?

Living in Berkeley, I encountered my share of crazies. They were treated benevolently by students because it was cool to indulge them. It's not a bad thing, of course, to show compassion. But this was different. Be nice to an insane person in front of your friends, and you're immediately seen as cooler than your less enlightened pals, as long as the scraggly behemoth doesn't jerk off in your eye. At times, students got injured because "out of the goodness of their heart" they tried to engage a "quirky eccentric." In Berkeley, this trait is known as "understanding." Elsewhere, it's called "asking for a poo sandwich."

I tried once to engage a homeless degenerate, whom I found daily, masturbating in my parking space, behind a dumpster, at school. I tried to reason with him. (I figured we had a lot to talk about.) He only disappeared after I dumped a bucket of warm soapy water on him from the roof, just as he was finishing. I took no pleasure in it, and if I did I would deny it anyway.

I recall such anecdotes because we need an antidote for the cool obsession with sickness. I do not mean your normal-definition sickness—like the flu, bronchitis, or even cancer—but serious mental illness that filmmakers and editors treat as a silent gift or some sort of romantic novelty, when they shouldn't. Embracing the mentally ill because you view the illness as a daring rebellion against the status quo helps no one and often leads to the emergency room. Or, in Hollywood, to an undeserved Oscar.

I am reminded of this as I stare at a recent cover of *Rolling Stone*, a magazine about as edgy as a Hula-Hoop. On the cover is Jon Hamm, the star of *Mad Men*—and get this, he's wearing sunglasses . . . and smoking! Yes, when you need cool shorthand for a photo shoot you bring in the heavy artillery of the unimaginitive: shades and cancer sticks. The look on Hamm's face is one of a man trying so hard to be cool, you might insist it's a parody. Then you read the caption that accompanies the image—"Don Draper Exposed—How Jon Hamm's Inner Demons Made Him TV's Hottest Star."

And there you have it: the "inner demons" BS that pops up whenever you need to apply artificial depth to an otherwise mundane subject. Actually, Hamm seems pretty likable, which should have been enough for a writer to illustrate. Either way, I went ahead and read the piece to find the cause of these demons.

I found lots of swear words, just enough to create a "bad boy" image for a TV star looking to dirty up his profile. Hamm lost his parents when he was young, which can account for melancholy (as someone who's experienced similar loss, I can vouch), but let's face it: Those aren't the inner demons we were looking for. Inner demons suggest wrenching torment, a secret dark side, a black soul. None of that, to the editor's disappointment, was revealed. So: No dark side? Dark glasses.

"Inner demons"—the real kind that cause actual problems— do not exist in sane people. Writers and editors know this. If Hamm actually had inner demons, *Rolling Stone* wouldn't go near him without a police escort. You know who has inner demons? Bona fide crazy people, like that dead freak in Florida who ate that homeless guy's face like a pot pie. Inner demons lead to external demons. But for people who traffic in cool, phony mental illness is an elixir put into motion to create entry points of intrigue. And cool. In real life, "crazy" equals serious injury, horrible hygiene, and incarceration. In *Rolling Stone*'s world, it equals cool. And painfully trite covers.

Magazine editors and their subjects aren't the only ones guilty of playing the "not everything is in good shape upstairs" routine. But it can only be played if everything else is in good shape otherwise. Meaning, ugly people cannot pull off the romantic, mysterious mental illness. That's why the Boston Bomber, not Fort Hood shooter Nidal Hasan, made the cover of *Rolling Stone*. If you're homely, you'd better just win people over with your down-home stability and common sense. Or be ridiculously rich. But if you're a gorgeous actor or a sexy singer, by all means play up the irrational, the dark, the unpredictable side of you. Destroy the furniture in your hotel, like Johnny Depp or Christian Slater did until they had finally created evidence for the press of their "dark, brooding sides." Destroying things makes you appear deep, which might lead to more substantial roles. It works—but only if you have dimples and carefully coiffed hair made to look unkempt. (It's a vanity I notice Angelina Jolie seems to have grown out of. Take note, Hollywood. It's called "growing up." It is possible.)

If you read any contemporary book or see any movie where the antihero is troubled, the troubling part (his mental instability) is usually fetishized instead of feared. Hollywood has now made it cool to be uniquely psychotic—to a point where people pride themselves on their quirky diagnoses. In Hollywood all instability is just a charming scene in *Forrest Gump*, *Rain Man*, or *Silver Linings Playbook*. The patient is sweet, goofy, or really good at blackjack. Unlike reality, they never shoot up a school or hack up their parents. Just last week, the brother of an old drinking buddy of mine killed their parents. He was a mentally unstable felon; he did not look cool. He looked like a mentally unstable felon. But if they make a movie about it, chances are he'll be played by Tobey Maguire, who is about as dark and deep as Lite-Brite.

In movies it's the crazies who are cool and the decent folk who are demonic. And what you end up with is a culture more fearful of institutionalization than the people who need to be institutionalized. Only in the counter-earth of Hollywood could such BS be pulled off with a straight face (which could explain the massive popularity of Botox).

Try to track down any opinion on the deinstitutionalization of the mentally ill, and you'll almost find a singular culprit: Ronald Reagan. Recently, ferocious frizzball Bette Midler blamed the Newtown massacre on double R, because he let all the crazies back out on the California streets around forty years ago. What's forgotten in all this is that the rise of patients' rights, combined with the softening glow added to the portrait of mental instability, made it impossible to help those who needed it by incarcerating them. I guess, of the two evils—mentally ill on the streets harming others versus mentally ill held against their will in hospitals—it was better to put the community at risk. Making the ACLU about as mentally ill as anyone out there.

So, why is craziness considered cool? Well, we like misfits. The idea of being an outsider creates a sense of depth that did not exist before. I love watching interviews of celebrities who say they were "outcasts" as teens, or "geeky" or even "ugly." It's almost certain that now, of course, they're tall, gorgeous, and successful. They want you to think they aren't just another pretty face—behind that pretty face is a sad clown, crying. Or perhaps self-mutilating or bulimic. All of which they'll be "raising awareness" about as soon as possible. I have a hard time believing that all of these irresistible beauties were repulsive shut-ins up until age nineteen. Especially since many are twenty-one now.

This is pretty harmless, if you stay far away from the harmful. The glorification of the unstable has given us a fair share of unnecessary exposure to really rotten people. As cool as you think unorthodox types are, there's nothing pleasant about the Manson Family. We can continue to elevate social deviance to a stature above your boring parents and your stupid siblings—but your boring parents and stupid siblings won't gut a pregnant woman in her home and then write mocking messages in her blood on the wall. Your boring family is almost always the victim in these horrible events.

The infatuation with the eccentric (a nice word for "batshit crazy") originates from a kernel of cool philosophy: Anything that rebels against structure has to be good. In fact, it has to be better! The white picket fence is just a symbol of oppression (it's white, after all); the man who tears down that fence is the hero. When a drifter convinces you to join his revolutionary group in the California desert, you can bet what's next isn't opening a frozen yogurt stand. More likely, it will be forced sodomy. But no matter. Cool makes evil just a part of the romantic resistance, and if you reject it, well, then, you're "the man" too. How many people lost their lives buying into an alternative lifestyle that defined itself against the repressive nature of contemporary society? (If you only count Jonestown, it's 918 members.)

Cool suspends critical thinking, the thought processes that can discern between good and evil—letting the harmful in. Be ing a dangerous asshole has somehow become an aggrieved group. I'm only surprised they don't qualify for subsidized housing. Oops, they do. See our prison system. According to the cool, those are no longer criminals—they're just victims of an unjust society railing against suffocating traditional norms. They are often "political prisoners." If you just got to know them better, you'd see that you're the problem. And when they rape you, it's probably your fault.

(If you get the chance, see a wicked little movie called *The Paperboy*, which details an infatuation between a flighty woman and a ruthless killer. She works tirelessly to free him from prison, and when she does, he ultimately, and brutally, kills her. That's the way it goes. Cool is nothing more than an avenue for the evil to trick the good into letting the evil in. This weird, messy little film should have won Best Picture on morality alone.)

What about actual crazy people? Does this romanticism of their predicament help? Hardly. As Heath and Potter point out, referencing the 1967 book *The Politics of Experience*, by R. D. Laing, the author maintained that schizophrenics weren't really ill but on "a journey of discovery." Discovery of what? The land of hallucinations and random violence? Translation: It's society's pressures they're reacting against, and their perceived illness is their way of breaking free from these evil structures that we've imposed against these deeper, more nuanced thinkers. We aren't cool enough to see how the illness isn't really an illness at all. It's just an alternative lifestyle—one that achieves more than our boring lives because it refuses to subscribe to our nine-to-five dreariness.

Never mind if the poor families dealing with the schizophrenic are going through an unmitigated hell trying to provide some peace for themselves and their tortured family member. What's important to the cool is that the sick person is the hero, and the people trying to help are the evil oppressors. "Madness itself becomes widely regarded as a form of subversion," write Heath and Potter. And subversion is always cool—regardless of the pain and suffering it causes others, or even the subverter himself. By this logic, Jeffrey Dahmer and Ted Bundy were just Elvis without the guitar.

It's dangerous to treat mental illness as a lifestyle rather than actually *treating* the mental illness. When the cool focus on guns as the impetus of violent acts, they avoid dealing with people who need help, who get those guns. We are a vast, rich country, with resources to care for those in need, but for reasons beyond comprehension we see treatment as an attack on individual liberty. We can no longer give people help, for it infringes on their freedom to be who they are, even if who they are might be a risk to others. So as talking heads rail against assault rifles to help their meager ratings, they avoid facing the uncool reality all around us: We fear to help the unstable few because it's cooler to let them roam free. Which is about the craziest thing you can do. The message delivered by Big Media every day, in a thousand differ-ent ways, is that it is better to be dead than intolerant. Lucky for them, messengers themselves are rarely being shot at or stabbed by madmen without provocation. Harvey Weinstein rarely takes the subway, I hear. He discovered there's no dining car.

ADDICTION TO ACCOLADES

A ward shows are funerals for the living. If you do not believe in God (and I veer in and out of that group depending on my success in finding a parking spot), then what replaces heaven? Fame. Fame is as close as you get to achieving immortality. Lots of people knowing you is the next best thing to a deity knowing you. Roughly one hundred years ago, the kind of fame we see now never existed. Sure, there was local fame, where the people in your village knew who you were because you happened to be really good at skinning an elk or cobbling a shoe. And there was the "legend" kind of fame—more like infamy—where the likes of Jesse James were known through gossip and pamphlets. But the kind of fame where a man born in Malibu is recognized by strangers in Tokyo—that never existed. Jesse James could still get a drink in solitude, provided he didn't wear a name tag that read I'M JESSE JAMES. (And, really, most fame occurs after death. Which is pointless, if you want to get laid now. No wonder the promise of "seventy-two virgins" is so necessary.)

But thanks to the invention of modern entertainment in the

form of motion pictures, we've created a new kind of sensation: the recognition by millions of *you*. (And it is *you*. You control their fame. If you just turned away from their needy grab for attention, it would be a different world.) Fame didn't figure into our evolutionary adaptations. I compare it to flying. People designate weirdos like me who hate commuting by plane as having a fear of flying. But "fear of flying" is nothing more than your evolutionary sense telling you, "This isn't where you, as a human, are supposed to be." (It's much the same feeling one gets in certain areas of New Jersey.)

Recognition by hordes of strangers is not meant to be, and when a person feels it, it's the same disorientation you would feel skydiving. Except it's way cooler. And for those rare few who experience it (I reckon there are approximately 74,500 famous people on earth—I've actually counted all of them, including Dana Perino, who counts as one-half), it diminishes the idea of an afterlife. The idea of an afterlife helped to cope with hell on earth. But if life on earth is heaven for the famous, then heaven evaporates. Heaven can't compete with the immediacy of instantaneous gratification. Fame is now the reason for life. And this mortal immortality, if you weren't a decent person before, will turn you into an asshole. Or worse, Barbra Streisand. We are now surrounded, outmanned, and outgunned by a generation of phonies, grasping for acceptance through appearance and behavior that have no productive impact on the world. It is all sound and fury, signifying nobodies. The key, of course, is to look good doing it.

A wards shows are those necessary oases that remind the chosen few that they are, indeed, famous. And cool. (As for my own fame, it is both late in arriving and appreciated. Fame at middle age is like discovering a whole new set of relatives you never knew but who know you. And they really like buying you drinks and asking you about Bob Beckel.)

The truly cool are people who work their butts off, heads down, unencumbered by desires for acceptance. Their success is based on achievement, not by external accolades. They know what they do is—if not great—at the very least their best, and reflects productive work. (If you've ever run into a military vet, you know *exactly* what I mean.) These are the people sitting in coach on a discount airline, trying to make it to their kid's soccer game before leaving again Sunday night on a business trip because the tickets are cheaper then. There are rare instances when this behavior results in fame: See the Clydesdale horses. And war. It is why, when I think of awards shows, I reverse Woody Allen's words, and say, "Maybe ninety percent of life is *not* showing up."

Yet, in today's culture, it is necessary to have more and more awards shows. These shows proliferate like rabbits on Cialis, and we watch them hoping for screwups, or at least something that makes us feel better about ourselves. But there are no awards shows for "best soldier" or "best mom"—or hell, "most effective urologist." Instead, they just get a coffee mug. Why does the army of the phony cool thirst so desperately for moments in which their activity is noted? Shouldn't what they do for a living be all that they need? It's the irony of the cool: Their bottomless pit of poor self-esteem demands a fire hose of complimentary speeches and trophies, or else they feel the very essence of this precious coolness fading. That's the secret Achilles' heel of the artificial cool: It's unsustainable without constant ego gratification. Once you no longer hear someone saying your name, you cease to exist (see *Estevez, Emilio*, or *Bieber, Justin—in six years*).

I hate to break it to you: You don't exist if this is how you measure existence. If you build your life around moments in which you possess other people's thoughts, you forget that those moments are temporary and vacuous. In a gawker's brain, when they see a person they recognize from "the television," it's never "My God, I love Adam Levine." It's "Look, it's that tattooed guy from that really shitty band!" Fame is not about liking someone— it's about recognizing them. There's a mile-wide difference there. When we see a recognizable face, we believe they are special and they believe they are special too. We think we know them, although to them, you are nothing. Or worse, someone from the Midwest who's probably not a vegan.

And part of being cool is being able to cultivate that stardom, then spend the rest of your life pretending to reject it. So you grow a beard, dress like a homeless person when shopping, or move to France (which I heartily endorse; please go).

In the world of pop stardom, what is mistaken for rebellion? A mediocre artist who spouts political beliefs that most freshmen in high school could have come up with after huffing Glade. How about railing against the Man, condemning suburbia or the sameness of that dreary suburban life, or ragging on people with boring jobs or nonglamorous lives? That's been a big, giant, clichéd part of pop culture. I hate it. Generally, what's derided among the coolerati is a simple lifestyle that 99 percent of history's humans would've killed for—and often did. What is derided is what keeps our horrible society together. You and me—we must mock this.

That's why I love heavy metal—it's about creating something majestic and sincere, the opposite of what the hip do with strats and skinny jeans. It is a pretty selfless thing, I think. I don't think the Melvins or Devin Townsend or Mike Patton care a single whit if anyone likes them. They work for a living. And they love what they do. The award shows—where none of them ever appear—are for those other artists who question whether they are liked or whether what they do is truly work. In short, so-called cool people need to be told they are cool. The rest just do their thing every day and know it works because it makes sense in their heads—and if they're lucky, make a living, feed their families, and hope the test comes back negative.

HOW MIKE AND CAROL

CRUSHED THE FERAL

For anyone born in the 1960s, all answers to life's problems can be found in one place: *The Brady Bunch*. The beauty of this wonderfully silly but often perceptive series is that, although it lasted only four seasons, it tackled every moral issue effectively and only once mentioned the word "sex." (It was the show when Bobby Sherman nailed Alice in the pantry.) It aired every Friday night, and I never missed an episode. Those were the happiest days of my life. Until I discovered NyQuil.

The lessons of the *Bunch* somehow stick with you forever. One episode still haunts me: season four, episode seventeen, called "Bobby's Hero." It aired February 2, 1973—an important time in our popular history, and mine too. I was nine years old, and approximately the same height I am now.

In this episode, Bobby, the youngest of the three Brady boys, becomes enamored of the lore of outlaw Jesse James, so much so that the ruthless killer becomes his hero, with Bobby playacting throughout, mock robbing and shooting his annoying siblings. It was an acting tour de force, as far as tours de force by freckle-faced freaks go (Danny Bonaduce never even got close). Why Mike Lookinland did not win an Emmy is a stain forever left on the fabric of Hollywood—a place where stains on fabric abound. I blame Cindy, evil spawn-of-Satan that she was.

Bobby's parents (the adorable Mike and Carol Brady) become concerned over this development and try to figure out a way to turn Bobby's infatuation off. In effect, they try to sober him to the reality of history. They want, in the words of one of the relatives of James's victims, to show that Jesse James was little more than a "mean, dirty killer," who shot his granddad in the back. They want to strip away the cool veneer and reveal the grotesque reality of a common, murderous thug. One far worse than David Cassidy.

But there was a problem: All the stuff in books and television portrayed James not as a killer at all but as a romantic outlaw. For a kid, Jesse James was cool because our culture made it so. Never mind the murders he committed; he lived outside our boring society, above the law, and did what he wanted. This was the definition of cool, not just for Bobby but for anyone enamored by the revolutionary groups erupting in the late 1960s to early '70s—from the Weather Underground, to the Black Panthers, to the horrible cast members of *Zoom* (precursor to the Branch Davidians). As long as cool is defined as anything but doing "what you're told to do by the man," then anything is accepted as laudable behavior. Killing becomes not a crime but an act of political heroism—a strike against a suffocating, corrupt world bent on killing your soul.

So being the great dad he is, Mike Brady does his research, finds a relative of one of James's victims, and brings him to their multilevel house, to give Bobby the unvarnished truth. (Okay, the show wasn't noted for its realism.) The relative, an old guy played by a great character actor named Burt Mustin, grimly retells how Jesse James shot his daddy in the back. He's sexy, in a male Angela Lansbury sorta way.

The story doesn't seem to shake Bobby. He still prefers to embrace the lies rather than accept the ugly truth of his obsession. It's not until Bobby has a nightmare, in which the killer murders the Bradys during a train robbery, that he changes his mind. (In the scene, actors use fingers as guns. I read somewhere that the directors believed guns would be too unsettling. Can you imagine?) This is the kind of remedy that comes from meeting a victim. It brings the horror home. I remember Bobby's dream as if it were my own. I remember being shaken by the episode, so much so that I didn't play cowboys and Indians for a month. I might be exaggerating. Either way, I took up hopscotch. Then, later, Scotch.

To this day, I always wonder why this isn't the law of the land. Celebrities and activists who adore violent radicals should be forced to meet the relatives of the people killed by those adorable violent radicals. Have Robert Redford meet the relatives of the victims of the Weather Underground. Let's see how brave the Sundance Kid really is. He certainly had no problem making a movie (*The Company You Keep*) based on those creeps. (I'll get to that in a sec.) Let the idiots who think the Boston terror bombing is a "false flag operation" meet the victims of the attack. They'd shit in their camo cargo pants.

In the 1970s, the glorification of rogue violence was no longer an exclusively male pursuit. The modern "you go, girl" sentiment was evident in the Manson Family, which had a fair contingent of young, vicious females. And even today, the violent female archetype is seen as cool by Hollywood's most vacuous minds. Director Harmony Korine put out a movie in 2012 about college women in bikinis committing crimes, called *Spring Breakers*. The plot is just an exercise in "hot moronism" (i.e., attractive people getting away with things that ugly people would be shot for). A drug dealer/rapper (played by the human comma James Franco) bails four female college students out of jail, which of course leads to a tawdry, repetitive crime spree. The hook to this flick was not just the plot but a gimmick: the casting of Disney stars Selena Gomez and Vanessa Hudgens in sleazy, non-Disney fare. It's like casting Barney the Dinosaur in a bestiality flick (which may happen—I hear he's broke). *Spring Breakers* covers all the titillating bases (sex, nudity, profanity, drugs), with nubile Disney lasses doing the dirty work. This is their way of closing a mainstream door while opening an "edgy" window. And it's a window to cool, which ultimately leads to nowhere. Or to Miley Cyrus and her vacuous, speckled tongue. Seriously, that's not a tongue, it's a European conger.

At least that movie was pure fiction—a product of a stale imagination. The worst kind of creation, however, is a fictionalized account based on true events. Translation: The director, unhappy about how the real events turned out, changed it to make it cool.

A recent example is Robert Redford's 2012 flick, *The Company You Keep*, based on the exploits of the Weather Underground—a group of sordid terrorists who tried to bomb the Pentagon, NYPD stations, Fort Dix, and the US Capitol in the 1970s. Through their own ineptitude, they killed a few of their own members (trying to make a bomb in a town house), but they killed innocent victims too. How is this portrayed in Redford's thoughtful flick? As a "thriller." Hmmm . . . I wonder who he's rooting for?

Here's the plot, as retold in the *New York Post* by Michelle Malkin (who nailed it): A robbery is attempted in the late 1970s by some made-up members of the Underground, who end up killing an off-duty cop in the process. Jim Grant, one of the terrorists, assumes a fake identity and goes on the run. The flick ends up being about Grant's struggle to free himself from his past. No doubt, it's highly sympathetic (I'm working here from a movie summary, for I made a vow years ago not to see any movies starring Robert Redford or Susan Sarandon unless they are documentaries that culminate in them being eaten alive in a vat of European congers).

Malkin contrasts the horrid flick with the facts, which will likely go unnoticed by the moviegoing public. Facts like these: In the real-life robbery on which the movie is loosely based, three innocent men were murdered in Nyack, New York—two cops and one security guard. Kathy Boudin and David Gilbert, the criminals, were sent to prison. Before this, Boudin was present when three people were killed after a homemade bomb went off in her house. She was paroled in 2003, after she was able to convince a sympathetic judge that she was also a victim, paralyzed by white guilt, which caused her to lash out at a society unfair to blacks. What's lost here: One of the men killed by the "revolutionary" was black. Malkin adds: "Waverly Brown served in the Air Force after the Korean War and had two grown daughters and a teen son when he died in the brutal shootout." The other victims left behind full families as well. Edward O'Grady and Peter Paige were also veterans, both leaving behind a wife and three kids. Nine kids, total, without dads. Thankfully, Redford's movie bombed. He deserves worse, really. He deserves to spend an hour stuck in an elevator with Waverly Brown's widow. Maybe he'd lecture her on climate change.

No one's heard from the victims again, but Kathy Boudin's brat son Chesa has done okay for himself. His adoptive parents are Bill Ayers and Bernardine Dohrn, also Weather Underground thugs and pals to the president. Chesa attended the best schools, feted by academia, which sees him as royalty. The odious off-spring still defends the thugs that are his parents. All in the name of fighting "US imperialism." Redford's fictionalized story adopts the same perspective: *Variety* called the flick, as Malkin reports, "an unabashedly heartfelt but competent tribute to 1960s idealism." (*There's* an endorsement—"competent.") It gets worse, with the paper adding, "There is something undeniably compelling, perhaps even romantic, about America's 60s radicals and the compromises they did and didn't make." I'd barf, but my vomit's too valuable to waste on this crap.

How does this poisonous, idiotic perspective still persist, when we can find the real consequences of such crimes through a basic Google search? Perhaps that's the engine behind this enterprise: People don't bother looking up the facts, at all. Certainly *Variety* writers don't. Rather than look for the real story, people watch the flicks that whitewash the story and prevent them from knowing what really happened. That's why Redford has no problem creating a fictionalized account. Because he knows no one will bother to research the facts, least of all the lefty media that adores him. In order to preserve the illusion that the 1960s and 1970s rebellion against societal norms was heroic, as opposed to toxic, this is what you have to do: Eliminate the truth and replace it with legend. You replace the gore with lore. And churn out vanity projects that attempt to preserve your cool as you enter your crusty seventies.

Redford's maxim is reflexive and predictable: When any organization pits itself politically (or even violently) against the boring and mundane structures that hold society together, you simply root for those who wish to destroy it. It's romantic, it's cool, it makes you appear thoughtful. When, really, it just makes you banal. And brutal. You are just another useful idiot, a pawn for destructive forces.

Which brings me to Angela Davis: Black Panther, Communist Party leader, and loving lackey to a murderer.

Angela Davis was a lover of George Jackson, a Black Panther party member accused of murdering a Soledad prison guard in 1970. Jackson had been in jail for five armed robberies and had spent a decade in jail before killing the guard. He became famous when his prison letters were published under the name *Soledad Brother*. Although as David Horowitz points out in his book *Radicals: Portraits of a Destructive Passion*, the letters had left out his delightful fantasies of poisoning the water system of Chicago (which is probably redundant). This was not a good guy. He was, in scientific terms, a bad guy. Pure evil.

During Jackson's trial, on August 3, 1970, Jackson's younger brother Jonathan invaded a Marin County courthouse armed with a pile of weapons. In the shootout that followed, two felons were killed, as well as the judge—his head blown off by a gun Davis had bought. Eventually she went on the run and became famous (and cool) as an international fugitive. She was a communist, feminist African American with an iconic Afro—all of which made her a hero of the New Left. Davis was put on trial for aggravated kidnapping and first-degree murder in the death of Judge Harold Haley. The trial ended in acquittal, for, as Horowitz points out, "the jury was stacked with political sympathizers for the accused." One of them, he writes, later became a lover of Angela's closest supporter. That's just a coincidence, a leftist might say, and if you disagree with him/her, you're probably just a hateful racist.

What became of Davis? You'd think her lurid offenses would

deem her untouchable. Not in academia. She went to where vicious left-wing criminals are always welcome: the faculty of a major university, the University of California, Santa Cruz. Her title? It's *awesome*. Professor of the History of Consciousness. I could not make that up if I was on six different types of acid. And she has been duly rewarded with commencement addresses and comfortable incomes far beyond the reach of your average prison guard or his grieving widow. How funny is it that academics decry a well-armed, law-abiding populace, yet embrace armed radicals with open arms? How funny is it that so many professors labeled Tea Partiers as terrorists, while kissing the asses of real, bona fide terrorists? It's not funny, really. But it's the result of a simple equation: One is cool, and the other isn't. Own a gun and keep it by your bed in your remote farmhouse? You're a redneck. Hang with murderous revolutionaries? Priceless. As long as you cling to cool, progressive beliefs that deem America evil, whatever you do is cool. Hell, you could nuke an orphanage and still get tenure.

But that's not the Jesse James moment for me. That comes later, as I read a recent interview on the Daily Beast website with Jada Pinkett Smith, a misguided actress, in a Bobby Brady sort of way.

Jada is now an executive producer of *Free Angela and All Political Prisoners*, which the Daily Beast effusively describes as an "in-depth and surprisingly revealing documentary that outlines the story of seventies icon Angela Davis." With that descriptor, you just know the article is going to be as balanced as a fat kid on a trampoline.

The documentary focuses on "the fascinating history of Davis's intellectual roots" and dredges up her "rarely discussed studies at the University of Frankfurt." Throw that garbage into the mix and she's no longer your average criminal, she's a deep thinker. Which excuses everything. Saying you studied at the University of Frankfurt makes your crimes so much more meaningful. I'm sure she knows how to say "shotgun" in German. After all, the best defense remains a good offense. No matter how offensive that offense may be.

Here's how Pinkett Smith describes Davis's relationship with the murderous thug George Jackson: "The love story gives you this entirely different view of the woman, her life, and who she was." I bet it's not a bad view either. Love is blind, of course, even if the lovers are the ones gouging out your eyes.

And here is her deft, intellectual summary of Davis's life: "She never apologized for her politics or her associations and she always looked fabulous doing it." The moral: As long as you look cool—and a "perfectly coiffed Afro" is cool—you can get away with just about anything. Being cool can turn a rampaging terrorist into a "political prisoner" faster than you can say "headless judge."

Like an educated, older, female Bobby Brady, Pinkett Smith swallowed the whitewashed fairy tale hook, line, and stinker, espousing the power of "change and political power." The reality just doesn't fit into this retelling, without smearing the cool veneer with the blood of innocents. So just focus on the fantasy.

The author of the Daily Beast piece refers to Davis's ability to be ruthless as an example of "stunning maturity." (Which the author of this book refers to as "stunning stupidity.") With that logic, I suppose the 9/11 bombers were the murderous equivalents of Mr. Miyagi.

But who comes out looking really cool in all this? Not only

Davis, of course. Pinkett Smith as well. She could have done a documentary on an amazing scientist, or a great teacher, but how would that help *her* career? It's just not cool enough. Revolutionaries make you revolutionary by proxy. I wonder if she's optioned the script on the Boston Marathon bomber. How can you resist his bedroom eyes? Yeah, he killed a few people, but he looked great doing it!

DOING THE WRONG THING

Probably the coolest thing ever created (besides medicated wipes) is rock and roll. The first time I heard it, it was as if a virus had entered my ear, rewired my brain, and made me forget everything I enjoyed prior to infection. AC/DC riffs obliterated youthful novelty songs and caused my brain—confused but enamored by this hormone-stirring music—to disown everything that used to make me giggle. Good-bye pajamas, hello pentagrams.

First and foremost, rock and roll is black music, and the only real evolution from rock and roll—hip-hop—is also black. Yes, I'm aware I'm breaking new ground here, but I'm getting to a point, I think. Bear with me, black readers about to throw up.

This is when a hack like me throws in a quote from a movie where a black character elaborates on my point. Here, a passage from the flick *Be Cool*.

> SIN LASALLE: Have you lost your mind? I mean, how is it that you can disrespect a man's ethnicity when you know we've influenced nearly every facet of white

America . . . from our music to our style of dress. Not to mention your basic imitation of our sense of cool; walk, talk, dress, mannerisms . . . we enrich your very existence, all the while contributing to the gross national product through our achievements in corporate America. It's these conceits that comfort me when I am faced with the ignorant, cowardly, bitter, and bigoted, who *have* no talent, no guts. People like you who desecrate things they don't understand when the truth is—you should say thank-you, man, and go on about your way. But apparently you are incapable of doing that! So . . .

[shoots his gun]

SIN LaSALLE: . . . and don't tell me to be cool. I *am* cool!

Yeah—what he said.

Now, I'm not saying cool didn't exist before blacks invented it. They just invented it *better*.

Think about what was epitomized as "cool" by white kids in the 1950s. James Dean? I remember him coming across as sulky—a walking pout, an A-ha band member in a tight T-shirt. And what the hell was he so cranky about? Guy walked through his life like his underwear chafed him. Jim Backus should've just slapped him and told him to "shape up!" (It worked for Gilligan.) Maybe blacks didn't become the touchstone of "cool" until a bit later. I'm not sociologically savvy enough to know, but rock and roll definitely had a part in it. Then white deejays grabbed it and delivered it to the white masses. From small clubs to stadiums, rock music changed what teenagers did with their free time and how they spent their money. Hence peace sign decals, posters by

Peter Max, and lava lamps (things no World War II vet would ever buy).

But cool, since then, has changed. Behaviors that are self-destructive at their core—criminality, illegitimacy, rejection of work—are not simply accepted, they are encouraged. And if these cool behaviors kill, as I believe they do, they kill nobody as much as they kill those who originally helped make cool ubiquitous: blacks.

What do I know? I'm a middle-aged white guy who listens to doom metal on a stair-climber. I'm no more an expert on black culture than Cornel West is on the Melvins. (Professor: Start with *Houdini*.) Ask me about Killer Mike and you might as well ask a four-year-old about German beer. (I've tried this—it doesn't work.) So I have to draw on my limited history, and scholarly journals I found on the Internet, to figure out a coherent point.

Let me draw on my past first. When I was a kid I had a best friend, who I'll call James (because his name was James). In kindergarten we got on like two peas in a pod. We weren't aware we belonged to different teams, with different skin colors. All we knew was that we laughed a lot, perhaps only because we sat next to each other. Really, that could have been it. When you're five years old and eat boogers for a living, you aren't picky (well, I guess you are, actually). I spent a year being friends with James. And then our friendship disappeared.

In first grade he went to one school and I went to another. When we ran into each other some years later (maybe sixth grade), he was different. I'd like to think I was the same (I'd grown an inch, but now I had a crossword of acne on my forehead and an unnatural obsession with Lee Majors), but he treated me oddly, not like an old friend but like a faceless ghost. A disposable stranger. To him, perhaps, I was suddenly just another white kid in a white world, and he was black. I didn't get it at first, but over time I sensed it had to do with me not being like him anymore. I accepted the new reality sadly, for no other reason than that there was no alternative.

His rejection bothered me, and I guess, since I'm writing about it now, it still does. Yeah, I know—when you're kids you don't know racism or the reality of life. But we were friends, and suddenly we weren't. For a forty-five-pound pile of good-natured energy, I was miffed. I was hurt. I drowned my sorrows in Mr. Pibb and Pop Rocks (together they give you x-ray vision).

I saw James a few years later. We were now officially strangers. On a few occasions, I would say hi, and he looked at me like I was a billboard for discount electrolysis. He walked right by me, cooler things in mind.

This episode with James was my first glimmer of a separation that became more common as I experienced more of life. If blacks believe we judge by color, why shouldn't they return the favor?

George Elliott Clarke, from Duke University, explains that cool, "though an amorphous quality—more mystique than material—is a pervasive element in urban black male culture."

He quotes other academics, Richard Majors and Janet Mancini Billson, who say that blacks employ cool "as a tool for hammering masculinity out of the bronze of their daily lives," or rather a way to "tip society's imbalanced scales in his favor." My take: If you are born powerless, you create your own power through a detached, "third rail" cool persona that others dare not touch.

It also means, quoting Majors and Billson again, that "coolness means poise under pressure and the ability to maintain detachment, even during tense encounters." I'd like to think that that was behind James's response when he ran into me, but maybe he just forgot who I was. If I go with the latter, I would have no chapter. SO . . .

These academics cite the dunking of basketballs, the end zone dance, and high-five handshakes as the epitome of cool. The "cool aesthetic" puts "importance of personal control over a situation," to a point that it "involves a willingness to engage in violence."

The other key element, which makes me think of my old friend who no longer acknowledged me, is detachment. With James that was the first sign that things changed, his decision to "suppress emotion," while valuing expressiveness and "verbal dexterity" elsewhere. In that sense, "coolness" means "cold." All of us do this—toward coworkers, relatives, and exes. But it's directed at *them*, not at their *skin*.

Coolness is a code that says, at least to me: "Greg, you are not part of my community, and for good reason." And this creates a force field that prevents dialogue between whites and blacks about the destructive behaviors that affect all of us, even if they harm blacks more. Whites cannot possibly discuss dependency, self-reliance, gangs, or lack of fathers without invading a space they believe they do not belong in.

How did something that seems positive (a dignified method of elevating you above an unfair surrounding) become purely a defensive reaction, for the sake of, well, being defensive? And what does being cool, ultimately, do to those who adopt the "cool pose"?

Research suggests it sucks in the long run, that it contributes to the underachievement of black children, boys especially.

I found a pretty interesting paper in the *Journal of Negro Education* (not my normal Friday night reading, but there you go). For those of you at home, the title is "Unraveling Underachievement Among African American Boys from an Identification with Academics Perspective," and the author, from the University of Oklahoma, is Jason W. Osborne. In it, you'll find out how acting cool ends up being a dead end for so many young, once-promising kids.

The cool pose often leads to "flamboyant and nonconformist behavior," which ends up, for its practitioners, as a road to detention, suspension, or expulsion in most schools. Being perceived as cool, for blacks especially, becomes incompatible with being a good student. Reading is for losers. Math is for geeks. Social studies is for both (i.e., me). Being highly motivated to excel in school is denigrated as uncool. To use the academic vernacular: "African American boys adopt a strategy for coping with their membership in a stigmatized group that is oppositional identification with academics," Osborne writes. In regular language: Book learning is for losers. It's not laziness. It's a determined effort not to be perceived as trying. The thing is, this pose is probably just as hard to maintain as working hard at something is. It's not lazy. Just wasteful.

The end result: Cool dictates that a large group of kids flunk out because it's uncool to try. Achieving success means adopting pursuits that are considered "white," which could lead to rejection by their friends. In short: School doesn't rate. It's just a game for whitey. Blacks aren't buying that road to success. The road is paved with an appeasement to lame authority with no promise of immediate reward. Better to shoot hoops and pursue rap— exhilarating areas far more amenable to black achievement (unless you count the New York Knicks).

What is a "cool pose"? Hell, how do I know? I'm about as cool as Jell-O. A cool pose for me happens when I'm alone, flexing in my bedroom while listening to Mannheim Steamroller. But Harvard professor Orlando Patterson, in a *New York Times* piece from 2006, describes the modern version in this paragraph:

> For these young men, it was almost like a drug, hanging out on the street after school, shopping and dressing sharply, sexual conquests, party drugs, hip-hop music and culture, the fact that almost all the superstar athletes and a great many of the nation's best entertainers were black.

Hell, even I admit that sounds pretty fun.

Returning to the denigration of scholastic achievements, he notes "that young black men and women tend to have the highest levels of self-esteem of all ethnic groups, and that their self-image is independent of how badly they were doing in school." In other words: they're failing but still feel cool.

There it is again, the bane of all existence: self-esteem. What I would give for a nation with low self-esteem. (I think it's called China.) Nothing bad ever comes from feeling bad, trust me. If I didn't feel bad, I'd get nowhere. The last time I felt really good and was completely stress-free, I was drunk. If I got drunk every day, though, I couldn't afford to get drunk. Feeling bad enables me to do the work that allows me, financially, to get drunk so that, periodically, I feel good. (That's pretty much a blueprint for life.) In the end the self-esteem movement only benefits the "experts" in self-esteem. They get book deals, TV spots, and academic grants. The rest of us get a generation of sullen blamers. It's beneath a lot of kids of every color to work at

McDonald's, yet they wonder why no one wants to hire them for anything else.

Patterson calls this cool adaptation "the Dionysian trap for young black men." But I might add that it's a trap for *all* men. It just hurts black men more because they're afforded fewer options for escape when it doesn't go well. A typical white kid can stop acting cool, and do something else, because he has the options to do it. And both end up working for the Asian kid who dropped the pose first.

And so cool culture has enlisted a generation of young men who need that decaying culture the least. It's a quickie feel-good antidote to a longer, harder path toward pride and self-respect; it cuts them off from the dedicated work that results in long-lasting achievement. Worse, it's so damn attractive that its destructive nature is clouded over by its appeal. And let's face it: It's fun. How do you fight that? Only one way—stigmatize it.

Because cool, for everyone, is a bad thing. It's a value-removal machine, a champion of reverse achievement. But, judging from recent history, for kids enduring the hell of inner cities, cool is worse. It's another version of crack. Offering immediate appeal and pleasure, it is a gateway drug to nowhere, a one-way ticket to the fruitless decades that follow. This is true not just for blacks but for everyone. What of white kids who start wearing their pants low and then end up having to drop their pants for *real* in prison? Every day I pray for the return of the belt.

We've come to a point where teens mock avenues that lead to achievement while they pursue roads to ruin. Evil finds the path of least resistance, and that path is almost always labeled "cool." Cool encourages the abandonment of effort that wins respect, degrees, and jobs. Cool allows evil in all its shapes and forms to take you to places you never thought you'd go. Or would want to go. If life offered mulligans, I'd bet every single person who opted for "cool" as a teen would jump at the chance to opt out of the lifestyle that swallowed a decade of their life, or more.

I wonder where the hell my old friend James is now. Unfortunately, statistics say that it's six times more likely that he'll be in prison than I will. That ain't cool.

KILLER COOL

If you're looking for the worst person in the room, find the guy wearing the "Free Mumia" button, as a show of support for a cop killer. Odds are he never wears that piece of flair around cops. That sort of brave political stand is better suited to a Bad Religion concert than a funeral for a fallen officer.

When I wrote this book, a homicidal maniac named Christopher Dorner was on the loose, somewhere in the mountains of Southern California. The former LA cop, Navy reservist, and murderer who was charged with killing three police officers and leaving three others wounded, posted a rambling "manifesto" elaborating on his murderous plans of revenge against a society that shortchanged him, a manifesto that also contained rantings about his favorite news personalities, politicians, and musicians. (I mean, couldn't he have just started a blog?) So, what do you do when a cop killer is also a cop? If you're a prick, you root for him!

I read his manifesto, fourteen pages that re-created the experience of sitting next to a caffeinated goofball on a bus who just saw an Oliver Stone movie for the first time (which is not much different from sitting next to Oliver Stone, actually). The diary was at times coherent, other times bitter, and the sum total of the mess was an angry guy with a score to settle, and perhaps suffering from an undefined mental illness. Sort of like an MSNBC anchor. In fact, exactly like an MSNBC anchor.

Nearly all of the asides in his screed, with few exceptions, were about news personalities. He adores Piers Morgan, making him the only person on the planet who adores Piers Morgan (aside from Piers Morgan). From his writing, it appeared that this nutcase had been stuck in a local airport where the televisions are all tuned in to CNN. I mean, when you are about to die, who thanks Soledad O'Brien and David Gergen? (Certainly not Jeff Zucker.) The guy actually wrote:

> Jeffrey Toobin and David Gergen, you are political geniuses and modern scholars. Hopefully Toobin is nominated for the Supreme Court and implements some damn common sense and reasoning instead of partisan bickering. But in true Toobin fashion, we all know he would not accept the nomination.

(Note: Representative of this guy's psychosis is that he actually thought there was a "true Toobin fashion," a reality break on par with admiring David Gergen, who may be Bigfoot after a good shave.) This drivel is toxic. Seriously, if this guy doesn't shoot you, he could bore you to death. Too bad he didn't read the thing out loud to himself first. He would have dropped dead.

Now this troubled vet is roaming in the woods, well armed and dangerous. Given his circumstances, I'm waiting for the White House, in the spirit of Benghazi, to arrest the producers of *First Blood*. After all, the guy who made the anti-Islam video blamed for the death of Americans in Benghazi landed in jail. You can just as easily blame Sly Stallone for this, as well as everything else that's occurred since *Cobra*.

Meanwhile nearly all the media covering the Dorner story avoids stuff in the manifesto containing pro-liberal sentiment. This is the same media that, when the Gabby Giffords shooting took place, immediately pointed fingers at Sarah Palin because of a graphic design element (a crosshair) on her website. You can bet if Dorner's manifesto had lauded the Tea Party, Piers Morgan would have been screeching at the top of his limey, affected lungs. Instead, the murderer lauds Piers, and he remains strangely silent, which in and of itself is kind of a relief. He's no Benny Hill. Point is: Dorner happened to like the right people.

More important, the psycho was a suspect in the murders of three people, including a police officer and the daughter of Dorner's former lawyer. You'd think every person on the planet would find this unacceptable, but you'd be wrong. Nope, this thug had a group of fanatical supporters all over the Web, populating Twitter with hashtags like #GodornerGo and #WeareallChrisDorner. Why the love? Rebellion is sexy. The idea that a man is on the run, battling this vastly bigger police force, seems cool. And for idiots living in an idiot culture, the actual victims of this coolness are quickly forgotten. No one really talks about all the innocents Che Guevara killed. Then they'd have to stop wearing that stupid fucking shirt. (But Che did us all two favors: One, he reminded us that anyone wearing a beret should be ridiculed; and two, he helped us quickly identify some of the true assholes among us. They're wearing Che shirts.)

Note: Perhaps the Twitter "We are all Chris Dorner" nonsense is actually accurate. Because if you're a jackass who falls for this shallow romance of evil, it does make you the same as the killer you adore. Well, maybe they aren't all Chris Dorner—they actually might be worse. They are Chris Dorner's *admirers*. Their own cheap, deluded values are actually *vicarious*. How many do you think were wearing Che T-shirts? And berets?

It is worth noting that when it came to killers like Tookie Williams and Mumia Abu-Jamal, it took some time for leftists to lionize the thugs. Now it happens in real time, before the guy's even apprehended, or even dead (which must be the "progress" part of "progressive"). Why wait until they get to death row, when you can be the first on your block to proclaim the innocence of a murderer? Now you can beat everyone in expressing your cool cred by proclaiming the innocence of a killer while he's actually still doing the killing. It's like watching *Dexter* without paying for Showtime!

About these morons who cheerlead death and murderers: It's really never about the killer. It's about them. It's about attaching themselves to a cause that separates them from others—that elevates them above the plebes who don't see the coolness of rooting for a thug.

As an experiment, I recently did a Web search for Daniel Faulkner. Who's that?

No one special. Just the police officer who Mumia Abu-Jamal shot and killed in Philadelphia in 1981. I googled Daniel Faulkner, and I got 193,000 hits. Then I googled Mumia, and I got more than 1.2 million hits. In mathematical terms, that's, like, a lot more.

Is it no wonder people flock to the thugs and ignore the real villains? It's easy when the skewed priorities of our cool culture shine the light primarily on the thug and not the victim. If you were some dumb kid doing a report for school on the Mumia/ Faulkner case, how could you not come away with a sense that

GREG GUTFELD

the killer was far more important than the innocent victim he killed? The victims are the first to be forgotten; the villain is the first to get a movie and a care package from Ed Asner.

Despite all the Google hits for Mumia, it would take less than an hour of searching to find out that Mumia killed a cop. But when you have the Beastie Boys behind you, all is forgiven. Ed Asner and even that former French PM François Mitterrand have his back too. Yeah, that assjacket Frenchie actually visited Mumia in jail. Imagine if George Bush flew to France to visit one of their more reprehensible criminals. (I was trying to think of an example, but could only think of Gérard Depardieu—who won't even live in France, even though French is the only language he speaks well, usually while drunk.)

What makes this hero worship more ridiculous is the new documentary on Mumia—which is about as balanced as a three-legged camel (my nickname), a vile valentine to a thug who masked murder as martyrdom. It's out now, to the gratifying pointless eyes of white leftists everywhere, who hope that the dangerous sheen of a murderer elevates their vapid lives. Mumia is global warming in a prison jumpsuit—cocktail conversation for cowards who want so badly to be cool.

This is why the Mumias and the Dorners get the love from the cool-craving chuckleheads in the media and elsewhere. It's not really about the killers, it's about impressing their peers with their shallow attempt at depth—depth defined by identifying with the bad guy and making the bad guy good. When you do this in movies, it's essentially harmless, because the victims are fiction. But in real life, every time you elevate a fiend, you denigrate his victims; you piss on the graves of the innocents and mock the unending daily horror of the families who must relive their loss every day.

Perhaps we should start a special bus tour, in which we take these gutless gawkers of gore to the victims' families' homes, where they can explain how sensitive Dorner really was. And if anyone accepts the invitation, pick them up, then drive the damn thing off the cliff. That would be totally uncool and wrong, I suppose. Maybe if I drive the bus, Hollywood will make a movie about me.

THE COOL'S WAR
ON WARMTH

For cool to exist, it must ignore all the boring stuff that made cool possible. We forget all the hard work that made our leisure time possible. We forget that our ability to go places, buy things, and listen to cool stuff is predicated on a population's ability to produce, to create, and to sell cool stuff. To gain that ability takes years of studying and hours spent not doing ecstasy at clubs or sucking on bongs in a basement, but alone, thinking, building, and working. Sometimes it's boring, sometimes fruitless. And other times it's ugly and dangerous, like war. We forget that without war we'd probably be nowhere. Without war—or the threat of it—the coolest among us would be hitched like Clydesdales to wagons pulling Vladimir Putin and the Ayatollah.

The beauty of progress is that it makes it easier for you to carve out a space to be nonproductive. Typically people fill that vacant leisure time with bad ideas that undermine any possibility for improvement.

If you're a college student who cannot see how the work of the uncool (the corporate shill, the businessman, the accountant) allows you to do all your cool stuff, then it's easy to condemn them. It's how you can hate coal, how you can hate natural gas while ignoring their roles in perpetuating your lifestyle. Every anti-corporate renegade with a Prius ignores the evil corporation that built the thing. The ugly stooges on evil corporate boards somehow have nothing to do with how you were able to fly to Cabo for spring break or heat your dorm room during an especially rough Boston winter. Your efforts of investigation cease at your dad's checkbook.

Campuses are rife with this apocalyptic ignorance: the idea that once you've gotten to where you are, it's time to pull the rug out from under the rest of the world.

I write specifically of the left-wing campaign to have college endowments divest their holdings in fossil-fuel companies because they have concluded that fossil fuels are evil. Fossil fuels are like the combustible versions of evil white men—they must be slain, despite everything they've made available to you. I have no idea why so many young people have a beef with petrified dinosaurs (the ultimate renewable vitamin). If I didn't know any better, I'd think it's an unnatural attachment to Dino from *The Flintstones*.

So far this divestment movement has spread to over 250 college campuses and they involve all the annoying players— the naive, the hipster, the nonhygienic (yes, I know that's redundant)—all joining sit-ins and building takeovers. If there ever is a time to sympathize with the lowly security guard making fourteen bucks an hour, it's during these exercises in petulance. Try watching a middle-aged black guy getting "informed" about the ways of the world from a dreadlocked twenty-two-year-old Caucasian grad student, egged on by a gray-ponytailed professor, and you marvel at his ability to refrain from strangling the student with his utility belt. The Stations of the Cross for the modern security guard can be found on every college campus: the trust fund kid, the weepy coed mad at Mom, the eternal grad student who smears the military while dressing in camo, head to toe. At least your average shoplifter at Walgreens isn't pretending to be anything else but your average shoplifter. The guard is just a man doing his job, trying to put food on the table for his family, yet he is less cool than the sniveling, soft-bellied student tempting him to break out the Mace, in an effort to ruin his life via YouTube. How many men and women have lost their jobs because they did what the rest of us would do: beat the crap—and there's a lot of crap to beat—out of these mindless, self-absorbed tools?

There are also hunger strikes. Hunger strikes are noble and sometimes necessary. If you're a political prisoner in China or North Korea (where the entire country is on a hunger strike, not by choice), I get it. For you, it's life or death. But at Harvard, it's about a press clipping and maybe getting a better grade or a higher class of hand job. So when an undergrad adopts a hunger strike in order to get someone to divest from oil, I say, let the twerp starve. Most of them are overfed, pudgy masses of soft tissue—it wouldn't hurt if these sad sacks lost a few pounds. They might even understand the plight of the average Venezuelan, who operates under conditions American activists see as utopian, when they're really nightmarish. How about the next time one of our coeds feels a hunger strike coming on, we exchange her with someone who's genuinely starving? In, say, North Korea or Saharan Africa? Might as well make it easy for them.

This divestment argument—once valuable when dealing with South Africa in the 1980s—has been co-opted by the bored and uninformed. If they were informed, and really cared, they'd fight against the injustices in countries where we buy our oil, like Saudi Arabia. They don't because in order to divest from those horrible places, we'd have to invest here and embrace fracking. It's weird how protesters were up in arms about apartheid decades ago but now are okay with far worse: executions of homosexuals, the stoning of rape victims, or even our casual drone program that includes American citizens as targets. Yeah—about that—the lesson here is that only a progressive could get away with that. An administration that had wanted to give protective criminal rights to enemy combatants from other countries now claims, as I write this, to conduct summary executions against Americans—radicals, no less!—utilizing drones without affording them anything remotely resembling due process. Their due process is disintegration into dust. (I don't pretend to care about them—Anwar al-Awlaki got what he deserved. But the hypocrisy is so breathtaking, you'd need a Buick-sized inhaler to handle it.)

And if these modern divesters were really informed, they'd see that oil, for lack of a better fuel, is the only thing we've got going. I know, I know—solar, wind, algae—that's the future. Sure. It was the future fifty years ago too. When is this future? Keep repeating that to yourself as you tap on your iPad, comfy in your heated local Starbucks. But if you took one moment to look around the world and see what the poor souls in other countries are heating their hovels with, you'd understand why coal is a lifesaver. For every life saved through carbon reduction, there are hundreds of poor souls dying from burning crap that's far more heinous than a Dave Matthews mix tape. (The fumes from burning them account for a million hospitalizations.)

But divestment, as always, is part of a larger, mustier idea, an old chestnut on our leafy, intellectually corrupt campuses: the dismantling of junk that works. I am willing to forgive students for not seeing this bigger picture—they're dupes in the game. And this kind of protest, really, is just something to do on campus before they get that summer internship at their daddy's law firm. The real villains are the folks running this game, and the Marxist professors that push it along. If only this were simply an attack on oil companies, but, as Stanley Kurtz points out in his great three-part series in *National Review*, the ideology behind it is built around returning America to a rural, foraging, agrarian, decentralized system of scavenging—with gardens on rooftops and huggable animals safe from the jowls of hungry stockbrokers. Which is when, I suspect, many of the rest of us will start dining on hipsters (they're not bad with mint jelly).

Whenever this preindustrial utopia is being discussed, real progress is always a marker for evil American domination. We have all the good stuff, and since we are evil, so is all of that good stuff we've made. I always wonder, if a twenty-three-year-old protester seeking the simple life suddenly finds out she has breast cancer, would she reject all that medical technology that a simple life cannot offer? If she sticks to her principles, she's in the morgue by twenty-four. There are no atheists in foxholes—and few Luddites in the dorms, when it comes right down to it. You can't play five seasons of *Breaking Bad* on a bong.

Let's examine who is behind the divestment movement. The major dude, Bill McKibben, is also behind the blocking of the Keystone Pipeline. When you see the same old faces attach themselves to a cause, you realize that safety, global warming, and toxic ponds have nothing to do with the greater aim. At its root, it's a strident ideology meant to dismantle an uncool world—one dominated by earth-raping monsters run by evil corporations (while also making tons of cash for Al Gore). And it's not that they want to return to a communal lifestyle; they just want *you* to. Communal in the end means coercive. Their desire to change your way of life is independent of the result. They really don't *care* if it works. What they want is what they condemn: power. Like Obamacare, their power is about limiting your options, because your deprivation is their victory. At least a greedy CEO's hunger for power might actually benefit a company and its shareholders. For these *eco-maniacs*, it's about subtraction: Your sacrifice enhances their power. It's the basis of all fascism, and ultimately ends in misery. Their real aim is scoring major cool points: The greenies gain a victory against the evil industrial complex that poisons hairless minority orphans. That's sure to get a movie made about them by Matt Damon, a movie no one sees outside Matt Damon's immediate family.

Despite the lack of practicality, the media finds the idea of foraging for vegetables on rooftop gardens to be delightfully cool. Reporters gladly type out pieces on such movements on their Macs, ignoring the fact that the people they pay tribute to are hypocrites. They want the iPod but not the power that makes it work. How does that work? Oh right, it doesn't.

Cool is the Trojan horse for coercion—it tricks you into giving up things you take for granted in exchange for the pleasure of feeling important. And whatever you give up is replaced by nothing nearly as efficient or affordable. It's a key lesson I've learned from the divestment movement: that the apostles of climate change were operating a ruse. This was never about a few degrees Celsius (a slight increase actually helps the earth; the warmer the planet, the less people die from the cold). It was about forcing the industrialized West to adhere to their preindustrial utopia. I say the "West" because I know these activists are smart enough to realize no one in China or Russia or India would fall for this shit. Your average Russian diplomat would throw you out a window during your presentation on algae. (Right after serving your eye-balls on a bed of caviar.)

Remember how the goal of your typical radical Islamist was to use terror as a means to return our sinful existence back to when Mohammed walked the earth? No technology; no television; no temptation. The only difference between them and these divestment dupes is that the radical Islamists cut to the chase by being horrifically violent. They learned to fly airplanes, instead of make flyers. The divesters want the same thing; they just aren't bloodthirsty. But they have a common enemy: America. They just can't get their act together between poetry readings.

In a way, I'd support the divestment, if only to watch one college—just one—actually give up reliance on oil completely. As I write this in January 2014, we are experiencing the coldest winter in decades. Do you really think these divestment dipshits are keeping warm with a solar panel and a copy of *Das Kapital*? Anyway, it'd be so worth it to watch students and their idiot pro-fessors freeze their commie asses off. They can burn this book to keep warm. Actually, they can burn thousands of this book. Contact me, guys. I'll give you a slight discount.

HOW HEATHENS BECOME HIP

The quickest way for a commie asshole to gain weepy fans is to die. This is something I'm willing to accept, as long as it happens regularly.

But it's no surprise that when someone truly awful dies, the cool break out in reverence. Which is what happened when Hugo Chávez croaked. On that day in March 2013, we saw a parade of misty-eyed celebrities and solemn left-wing hacks paying tribute to a dead guy. Out of the woodwork came a parade of Hugoslavians, tyrant-lovers who could overlook the heathen's badness for the sake of coolness. See, someone can be truly evil. But if that person runs a country and *you know that person* well, it makes you kinda cool. It's better to know Darth Vader than Doris Day. It's pretty cool to brag that you just shared a burrito with a murderous despot, as opposed to a biscuit with Billy Graham.

And so when Chávez bit the dust, who did we see? Sean Penn. Oliver Stone. Jimmy Carter. Joe Kennedy. All decorating the corpse with wreaths of blithering blather. And no one blathers blitheringly like that quartet. That's the worst set of four since the last Who reunion.

As *USA Today*, a paper one finds sadly staring at you from your hotel room doormat, reports, an emotionally upset Sean Penn mourned the death of the fifty-eight-year-old socialist creep. Sean wrote in a statement sent to the *Hollywood Reporter*: "Today the people of the United States lost a friend it never knew it had. And poor people around the world lost a champion." He added: "I lost a friend I was blessed to have." Penn needs to tell you that he knew the guy. A world leader. That's cool. I guess playing Jeff Spicoli and marrying Madonna wasn't enough (one made your career, the other ruined your urinary tract). Yeah, this is the same chap who told Piers Morgan that Ted Cruz should be institutionalized. Talk about the pot calling the kettle batshit crazy. If Penn got any nuttier, he'd be a Snickers bar.

Of course it would be uncool to point out to Penn that Chávez was no champion of the poor. Under his rule people became far poorer in Venezuela. And in the midst of an oil boom, Chávez engineered a murder boom. The murder rate in his country tripled during Chávez's tyrannical tenure, hitting a high of 67 per 100,000 residents in 2011, compared with a murder rate of less than 5 per 100,000 in the United States (and that includes Baltimore). And about 10 or 20 less than the last Penn movie.

Penn was joined, per usual, by director Oliver Stone, who said, solemnly, somewhere: "I mourn a great hero to the majority of his people and those who struggle throughout the world for a place." He added: "Hated by the entrenched classes, Hugo Chávez will live forever in history.

"My friend, rest finally in a peace long earned." This is from an *adult*, mind you.

And no list of apologists for evil is complete without Michael

Moore. This nugget comes from the *Michigan Live* website, which reports Moore praising Chávez in a feeble collection of Twitter messages, on the night the Venezuelan viper expired.

> Hugo Chávez declared the oil belonged 2 the ppl. He used the oil $ 2 eliminate 75% of extreme poverty, provide free health & education 4 all.

> That made him dangerous. US approved of a coup to overthrow him even though he was a democratically-elected president . . . You won't hear much nice about him in the US media in the next few days. So, I thought I'd say a couple things to provide some balance.

Save the balance, Mike. You need all you can get just walking across the street.

When you desire to be the coolest person in the room, you also become a willing dupe. The great writer Michael Moynihan calls it the "free breakfast" theory of tyrant love. All an evil scumbag has to do is offer something seemingly free, and somehow celebrities forgive all the other awful things they did. You raped my sister but bought the city a pig? It's a push.

For Chávez to obscure his attack on the poor, he had to brand himself as the champion of the poor. Which is why he scored an amazing amount of free press, delivering free heating oil to America's poor. "Even if it was political opportunism, as conservative critics insisted, it got home-heating fuel to hundreds of thousands of yanquis during the past four winters, when the price was often skyrocketing," *Time* magazine's Tim Padgett reports. (By the way, how is "yanquis" not racist? I'm *enraged*!) Too bad Chávez couldn't lend a hand to his own people—but they were far less important than the accolades to be gotten from the American media.

Meanwhile, the *Huffington Post*—the beehive for boneheads—writes: "Hugo Chávez was a man of many talents: he played ball, sang songs, pulled out pistols, and got down and groovy—and that is precisely how we'll remember the Venezuelan leader."

Precisely? That he got down and groovy? What is this, *Soul Train* for psychos? Operating in the lurid lexicon of cool, one must forgive tyranny because the guy knew how to party! It makes you wonder how the Huffpo would have covered Hitler's death if he had only mastered the bongos. If only Stalin did karaoke! If only Pol Pot was a Doors fan. Didn't Idi Amin love to slam dance?

There were others involved in this freakshow tribute, including the embarrassingly self-absorbed British politician George Galloway, who called Chávez a "modern-day Spartacus." Galloway, mind you, never met an anti-Western tyrant he wouldn't swap spit with. To him, radical Islam is a justifiable response to our own evil. Make a deal with the devil, and maybe the devil will kill you last.

But the real champion in this Hugoslavian hug? A nobody at *The Nation*, a guy who gives GGs a bad name. His name is Greg Grandin, and this is his take:

> The biggest problem Venezuela faced during his rule was not that Chávez was authoritarian but that he wasn't authoritarian enough.

Tell that to those who didn't survive Chávez's horrible rule. They won't hear you, because they're dead. Hmmm . . . if only Stalin was more efficient, the world would be a better place. (The population would definitely be more manageable, that's for sure.) Great job GG; you win the Walter Duranty award for advocacy journalism. It looks just like an Oscar. Only the figure's head is up his ass.

While it's unseemly to rag on a dead guy, there's something equally off-putting about lionizing a bad man. At its heart is a petty, shallow jab at America, the Goliath. And why? After all, Americans aren't bad people. We're just good people who do good things really well. And we do screw up now and again, but all in all, we get things right. We're kinda awesome, history attests.

But American goodness is a boring, uncool concept. Instead, among the cool kids in this vacuous universal high school, the default cliché that infects all thinking comes down to "us evil, them good." Paying tribute to Hugo Chávez translates into, "You Americans are too big and bad to understand the plight of the common man." The cool don't consider that this "common man" was hoarding billions of dollars, allowing criminality across the country, and fostering a murder rate that outstrips countries involved in actual wars. Or that America was built by common men. Successful common men whose only fault was that they weren't non-Caucasian leftists.

When Oliver Stone and Sean Penn pay homage to a man who considers the United States the cause of all the troubles in the world, their conclusion is simple: We agree with the dead man—America sucks. This cool perspective might help a drug-addled actor score a dopey model at the bar. But it makes everyone else familiar with history throw up.

So the next time you run into a cool person who finds it cool to deify a dead creep, ask 'em this: Should your cool assumptions about the flaws of America excuse your allegiance to a thuggish critic of our country?

Venezuela might have the world's largest oil deposits, yet most of the country's citizens are mired in poverty. Chávez died a billionaire. How can you laud this fraud—a one percenter if there ever was one? How can you say he was good for the poor? If he's good for the poor, so are hepatitis A, B, and C. This is a country so screwed up, they put price controls on toilet paper. This poses quite a risk, since Chávez fans like Penn and Moore are so full of shit. They're Porta Potties on legs.

Another question to ask: How do you think this cool pose is viewed by folks who escaped the real, authentic horror of dictatorships from hellholes in Africa or the entirety of Cuba?

How do you explain the praise heaped upon a man like Chávez, who controlled the media, banned free expression, and imprisoned those who spoke out against him? Do you think Penn, who loved to visit the despot, thought it was simply too rude to say something when he was there? As an invited VIP guest, he didn't want to upset a famous friend? Do you think he knew those trips were prepared for him? These primitive attempts at Potemkin villages, where potholes and rocks were painted over to create a joyful facade over the country's decrepitude? Do you think Penn knows what a Potemkin village is? He probably thinks it's a retirement community in Florida (where Madonna is living).

Why do we have champions of tolerance asking that we tolerate those who traffic in intolerance? Wouldn't it make more sense to salute those who challenge a man who attempts to monopolize the media, while nationalizing every industry he can get his grimy paws on? Isn't that speaking truth to power? If Bush had done what Chávez had done, how quickly would these cool creeps be handcuffing themselves to the White House fence, spray painting their torsos with theater blood, the cocaine still searing the lining of their sinuses?

In truth, these apologists for evil are far from cool. They are losers, shams, frauds. Worst of all, they are predictable. The obvious hole in their respective souls drives them to embrace the world's worst ghouls. If only to mask an unhappy reality: that they're all just boring sacks of aging bones and irrelevant beliefs. As we all are. But at least most of us don't fall in love with dictators.

At Hugo's funeral, you saw Iran's hirsute hothead Mahmoud Ahmadinejad shoulder to shoulder with our own Secretary of Stupid Sean Penn. Jesse Jackson also paid a visit, which seems odd, priority-wise, given the state of *his* family. But they all hit the same red carpet (fitting that it is red—as a tribute to the country's murder rate). Maybe this will turn out to be an adult moment for America, when we stop and wonder if following the cool is the right thing to do. This naive embracing of anti-American bullies seems purely adolescent—a desire to thumb your nose at evil Daddy.

But while being callously cool means mourning the death of thugs and fraternizing with our country's enemies, it also requires celebrating the death of someone great. Just weeks after Chávez, Margaret Thatcher died. Before the news sank in, the ghouls were already in the streets celebrating, in force. Impromptu street parties popped up in Glasgow and London, with drunken yobs stumbling through the streets, holding all kinds of sinister signs, rejoicing in the death of Maggie as they shat their pants. On Twitter, as always, the ghoulishness is amplified, because it's anonymous and easy. When a British celebrity (a Spice Girl whose name escapes me, and probably her) expressed sorrow over Lady Thatcher's demise, she was met with vile slurs (all of which rhymed with the word "bunt"). The second-most trending topic on Twitter was "no state funeral." Amazing. From the very people who want the state to pay for everything else. If Churchill were alive, he'd slap somebody. Probably everybody.

But because the left thinks the right is evil, and they believe the prime minister is a monster, their vileness is sanctioned. Their ghoulishness is coolishness. Their celebration mimicked those in Libya after Gaddafi croaked. But the Bedouins had better hygiene.

When I looked at all the footage of the partiers in the streets, I could not help but notice that they were young. They had zits. And iPhones. These dolts were way too young to remember Thatcher, who was less a "warmonger" than the Austin Powers lookalike who came after her. All this vitriol was emanating from students—all stuck in that Hacky Sack socialist mind-set. The *Daily Mail* reported on the National Union of Students conference in Sheffield, where some delegates actually cheered when told of Thatcher's death. I'm sure they were cheered, in turn, for their cheering. Then they went back to reading the *Guardian* in their underpants, listening to Moroccan Dubstep, and waiting for "Mum" to serve beans on toast.

So why such hate, from people who only knew Thatcher by grainy pictures of her in the paper? Well, if you swim in the sewer, you're going to come out stinky.

And that's your typical product of academia these days, soaking in a scholastic cesspool where the coolest thing you can do is crap all over the West and its glorious achievements. An anti-West relativism—that banal evil that infects every corner of your average campus—makes it totally acceptable to view Thatcher as just another Hitler. And to believe the West is no better than its enemies. For a cool student, hating America makes them cooler. It's like saying you're with the band. A shitty band. Think Maroon 5 with a better singer.

A MAGAZINE FOR
MURDERERS

If only bin Laden had been younger and hotter. If only he'd had *abs*. Then Jann Wenner, publisher of *Rolling Stone*, who put the Boston Bomber on the cover of his rag, might have done him first. But the Boston Bomber cover proved my book's premise: The moral bankruptcy of the cool culture makes evil attractive and decency boring.

The cover featured the bomber as a delightful, doe-eyed ragamuffin. It was a shocking cover, in that you were shocked as to why a once-venerable publication would choose that picture—one that mocks the dead and their suffering families. I don't think that's the kind of "shock value" Wenner had in mind. For shock to have any "value," it has to contain some truth. This was shock for shock's sake—and its message seemed to be, "Look how cute this kid is. He can't be that bad, can he?" If you didn't read the article and just went by your gut response to the cover (revulsion), you'd be right and save yourself an hour.

But I read it anyway.

I do not subscribe to *Rolling Stone*, for I find it a sad, laughable shell of its original being. I used to adore the rag. The beautiful cover of Joe Strummer and Mick Jones of the Clash adorned my teenage bedroom wall for years, until it evaporated into a desiccated shroud. When a favorite band made the cover, you were happy for the band and for yourself—because your tastes were validated. I felt the same way when they put Cheap Trick on the cover. But not when President Obama appeared. (I had no idea he was in a band!)

More recently, I would buy the magazine when I needed something to read on a flight. When zonked out on Xanax and a glass of wine, forking over five bucks for some inane editorial seemed entirely appropriate. The writing was as mushy as my brain matter. The magazine is so incredibly stupid that I need to be stupid to absorb it.

Now, however, I cannot look at the magazine without sensing a corpse. A dead, lifeless product. As I write this, Bob Dylan is on the cover. I cannot even look at it. And he's a great man, with decades of great achievements behind him. He's also a smart man, and I'd like to read what he's thinking. The man loved Barry Goldwater for Chrissakes! But it doesn't matter. I can't get that bomber cover out of my head. And it's not Bob's fault. It's *Rolling Stone*'s. I compare it to food poisoning. I used to love lamb kabobs. I'd get them before taping my late-night show. Then one night I got sick to my stomach. It might not have been the kabob's fault. It could have been the quart of cough syrup. But I threw up so many times I could have qualified for Fashion Week. Once I recovered, I never had lamb again. That's how it is with *RS*. They poisoned me once. Never again.

I am not saying I decided to boycott the mag. I hate boycotts. I stopped buying *Rolling Stone* because I decided I no longer wanted to contribute to an engine that elevates evil. Placing the bomber on the cover gave his fans something to frame. It awarded him the pinnacle of fame desired by so many losers today.

Which leads me to another reason why I no longer buy *RS*. They *don't* want me to buy it. This is no epiphany, just a reminder that liberal magazine editors *hate* America. They think the rest of us are stupid, narrow-minded idiots who don't understand the injustices of life. So if they put a bomber on the cover, and we don't like it, it's obviously *our* problem. They might express some regret over the fallout (and the millions of dollars lost from fleeing advertisers), but secretly that cover was a "fuck you" to everyone who doesn't live on a coast or who thinks Sarah Palin is probably a decent chick.

The bomber cover, in all its glossy, curly-haired adorability, validated doorbell-ditch terror as an alternative path to stardom. To be a different kind of rock star. You can truly rock the world, with explosives. It used to be bad to "bomb" as an artist. Now the artist is the bomb. Dzhokhar Tsarnaev is an explosive talent, the kind that costs an arm and a leg.

For the purposes of a *Five* monologue, I read the entire cover story as research. And afterward, I threw up. But also, I sensed that those who defended the cover were way behind the times.

Their only real point was to show that terrorists no longer have to look like terrorists—they can look like members of One Direction, the latest incarnation of the ubiquitous, adored-by-millions boy band. (If you aren't familiar with the band, they're toothy lollipops with hairpieces.)

This idea—that evil can be elegant—was apparently a revelation for the magazine's lame editorial staff. For the rest of us, it was old news. Come on. We've known since we were kids in

Sunday school that bad can be beautiful. Many of Josef Mengele's surviving victims described him as "handsome" and "distinguished." It's old news—evil comes in many forms. Including *Rolling Stone.*

Isn't that the point of the whole Adam and Eve story? Eve chose a fruit, not a rutabaga. Had any of the *RS* editors heard of Pretty Boy Floyd? He had that name for a reason. He was pretty and boyish. Like an old-school Lena Dunham with a five o'clock shadow. And what of Ted Bundy? His aesthetically pleasing visage enabled him to rape and mutilate countless females. The idea that evil is always ugly is held only by the profoundly naive.

Perhaps the writer assumed all terrorists are homely. That seems a tad bigoted. Maybe it's that prejudice that causes average-looking men to become terrorists!

Or maybe Middle Easterners just aren't the writer's type, but this Chechen bomber is. Perhaps she thought she might have a shot with him. He is single after all, and being in prison for the rest of his life means you'll always know where he is. Not a bad catch for most *RS* editors (Jann included).

The real epiphany: By placing the bomber in a flattering light on their cover, they had inserted sickening evil into the clichéd "bad boy" mold. This "guy who makes your dad nervous" stereotype is the backbone for all stories on renegade rock stars and "unstable" actors and pop stars. We've seen this, from Brando to Bieber. Now, the pretty boy is a bomber. That's what I would call a shift.

The *RS* piece on this punk broke less ground than a rubber shovel. The template for such pieces is this: [Insert name of artist] is so dark, so mysterious, so "other" . . . yet he's also irresistibly sexy. His darkness invites you to know more about his secret torment, and his boyish good looks plead for your desire to connect. Maybe you could change him!

On *The Five*, I ran through a list of actual descriptors of the bomber, from the article. They included:

- ▸ beautiful
- ▸ tousle-haired
- ▸ a gentle demeanor
- ▸ soulful brown eyes
- ▸ smooth
- ▸ a golden person
- ▸ pillow-soft
- ▸ a great three-point shot
- ▸ a diligent student
- ▸ just superchill . . . really humble
- ▸ girls went a little crazy over him
- ▸ "so sweet. He was too sweet . . ."

Christ, this reads like the notes left from classmates in your freshman yearbook: "Jasmine, like U were so cool!!! XOXOXOX! Super meeting ya & can't wait till we hook up over Summer! Let's chill!"

When you run through those attributes, the article becomes more than a fantasy confessional. It was a pathetic plea for easy compassion from people who had little connection to the actual tragedy.

In sum, the writer devoted thousands upon thousands of words on a mass murderer. Because, in the hearts and minds of editors, he's just more interesting than his victims. What can you say about the victims, other than, "It's horrible they are dead"?

But with the killer, you can go on, for, like, ever. More words have been devoted to the John Wayne Gacys of the world than the victims of such monsters. They're cooler, editorially speaking. No wonder the networks are flooded with shows about brooding, complicated serial killers. They're so . . . deep.

Which is why this article will generate more marriage proposals from women than a seventy-five-year-old chain-smoker winning the lottery.

I wonder if she would have described the bomber in similar terms if he had been a member of the Tea Party. (The profound idiot David Sirota actually pleaded for the bomber to be a white right-winger. I felt bad for his therapist when it didn't happen.)

If Tsarnaev had been a Tea Partier, you can bet Cher's tapeworm that the story would have been treated differently. Instead of being about the bomber, it would have been about how this right-wing bomber represents a greater, more destructive movement growing within America. But because he's actually an Islamist, he's treated like an anomaly, a mysterious aberration one must analyze with thought and feeling. If he had been a Tea Partier, though, he would have been a symbol of so many like him that lurk in every Walmart aisle. He would represent the Republican Party, the viewers of Fox News, or anyone who didn't vote for Barack Obama. He would be me, after four drinks.

Some people admired the detail (which passes for journalism these days at *Rolling Stone*) found in the piece, and I don't deny its meticulous devotion to adjectives. But it camouflaged the real point of the article: how modern corrosive pop culture can soften evil through the easy prism of cool. Good versus evil becomes irrelevant as long as you master the look of cool. If you're cute and dangerous, those evil deeds you perform become secondary. Blown limbs are no match for blown hair. Too bad Nidal Hasan didn't look like Russell Brand. Jann would have done a centerfold. Even more, if you're a mediocre musician with no buzz but great cheekbones, maybe terror beats giving guitar lessons to middle-aged accountants in your rented basement apartment.

This kind of thinking survives as long as the cool's own, comfy survival is not under threat. If the *Rolling Stone* offices had been the target of bombing, would they have put such an adoring photo on their cover? If a majority of their staff had lost their arms and legs, would they still have had the heart to do such a thing? Something tells me the cover would have been a graphic depiction of their blown-out, blood-spattered offices. But since they were not targeted, they embraced the lilting, longing look of the perpetrator and his troubling dissatisfaction with life in America. You could never do that if your underlings—those employees required to put out the rag—were currently being fitted for prosthetics.

Lucky for editors of pop culture rags, terrorists never target their admirers. They know better. Even evil knows the negative value of bad PR.

And it is that knowledge that allows evil, in all its forms, to persist. Cool, by definition, exists as opposition to the boring, an antidote to the traditional things we've been instructed by the superficial coolies are laughable. It's something *Rolling Stone* has trafficked in for decades. It's better to be bad and cool than good and uncool.

And in the case of the Boston Bomber, they revealed such ideology for all to see. It diminishes the impact of suffering of others, in the service of succulent novelty. The cool does not provide an excuse for evil; it gives it a bistro to relax and execute its plans.

When you have enablers of evil like *RS* willingly playing the dupe, you realize how far the cool have come in pushing for our own, inevitable demise.

Rolling Stone has shown us that the philosophy of cool is no longer cool. We have found them out. We're on to their game and are tired of a scam that sees suffering as a collateral prop for a vacuous ideology. We are no longer suckers for a nice picture. And we have better things to do with our money than spend it on a rag that seeks to explain away evil.

Me, I'm getting a subscription to *Cat Fancy*. When was the last time a cat blew up anything?

But *Rolling Stone* isn't the only guilty party that romanticizes evil. Turn the page, and you'll find enough to fill a marathon. (That's called a tease, people.)

SONNETS FOR TSARNAEV

It is the terror that dares you not to speak its name. Yet radical Islam screams it, *over and over and over again*, often before open firing. It's just that our media, our academics, our politicians refuse to hear it. To the cowardly cool, terror is just two words: Timothy McVeigh.

Who commits most acts of terror these days? Better not ask that, for you will find the answer to who bombed Boston faster than anyone else (certainly faster than the FBI). And be labeled a bigot faster than Phil Robertson at a GLAAD rally. Better to speculate about everything but the radical Muslim elephant in the room.

When terror struck the Boston Marathon on April 15, 2013, the cool sentiment from the cool jackasses in the media and beyond spewed forth like raw sewage—linking the attack to anything but the most obvious truths. Their initial response to terror: to go after people you disagree with politically.

We saw that on April 15, when a slew of journalists, among them Chris Matthews and Nicholas Kristof, did exactly that.

(Kristof at least apologized for initially blaming Republicans for the bombing; maybe his bosses at the *New York Times* thought that was too much even for them.) One anchor named after a wild canine initially linked the bombing to Tax Day; a fat celebrity snidely put it on the Tea Party. And there were those who openly prayed that the killers would be white Americans. At a certain point, even if you get paid to pontificate, you might want to just hold your tongue for maybe a day or so. Or better, a decade or two.

The day after the attack, blogger David Sirota wrote a piece for Salon titled "Let's Hope the Boston Marathon Bomber Is a White American." At least he was honest.

Sirota claimed that our own racism and Islamophobia would cause us to ignore a bomber's background if he's white, thereby reducing our outrage and its violent consequences. But if the bomber turns out to be Muslim (which is what happened), we'd react differently.

So he really wanted those guys (or gals—we can't be sexist here) to be white Yanks. Which makes you wonder: Did he mean white people, like the white people of Occupy Wall Street? Some are currently on trial in Cincinnati and Cleveland for terrorism, after all. Or what about the retired terrorist Bill Ayers and his horrible wife? They're white too. They make me ashamed of my race. The human race, as the old saying goes.

Something tells me, though, that that's not the kind of "white American" Sirota had in mind. He was speaking in code. His "white" really meant conservative. My gut says he had been praying that the bombers were those phantom Tea Party extremists we keep hearing about but never see. How grand his life would have been if he had been right! Instead, he's been exposed as a fool. And he probably feels worse about that than anything.

Why do the likes of Sirota write such drivel in the first place? Perhaps he had trouble fitting in as a child. Or he was pressured into it by an older brother (both excuses used by the press to defend the acts of one of the bombers). But the real reason is obvious to anyone who's had to endure the presence of academics and media hacks at social gatherings. It's cool to have a low view of Americans—not its enemies. You get paid to express such opinions because everyone around you thinks the same way. This is the cool creed: When bad things happen to America, think badly of America. Michael Moore is the king of this. Here's what Moore tweeted when the bombers were found to be young Chechen radical Islamists:

> Breaking: "Two Americans Bomb Boston Marathon"— both Tsarnaev brothers were registered voters and US citizens. #restofworldyouaresafenow

Yippee, I guess. He will grab any straw but the one in front of him (unless it's firmly stuck in a milk shake).

Of course the terrorists are white. But if they were white Christian conservative Tea Partiers, Michael Moore would be shouting it from the rooftop, if there was a freight elevator sturdy enough to get him there. But now that we know they are Muslim, we are told not to jump to any conclusions or point out the obvious, predictable trend. That would be wrong, and bigoted. So let's get this straight: It's okay to smear a right-winger if you think they did it. And once they are vindicated, it's still okay to smear a right-winger (because you wanted to think they did it).

This reaction on the left was downright common. They hadn't been this disappointed since it turned out bin Laden wasn't a Mormon.

GREG GUTFELD

W hy is it that after every act of terrorism, there seem to be loads of angry leftists angry at people who didn't bomb anything? Yes, I'm conservative. But why the hell are you yelling at me? Wouldn't it be nice to see the big names who linked all of this to taxes and Tea Parties and abortion come forward to admit the real motives? Never. It's just bad taste to talk about such indelicate matters. If only Palin had had a #crosshairs symbol linked to a map of the marathon, this could all be different. And so much simpler for Wolf Blitzer. (I guess it's tough to be measured when your name sounds like a video game.)

So what do the cool kids do when they're wrong about terror? When an arrest is made and we find out that the scumbags were Muslim radicals? Well, they never admit they're actually wrong. Instead, they resort to their fanny pack of ready-made justifications. The first one is always relativism: They say Islamic terror is no different from, say, an abortion bomber. Or that Islamic extremism is no different from any other kind of religious extremism. In order to make this equation work, however, you must be really bad at math and history. Or you sat next to me in high school.

Make way for "root causes," a cool response to evil if there ever was one. "Cool," after all, is defined as being detached, unconcerned. And if you want to detach yourself from true evil, simply focus on the personal turmoil of the bombers, which allows you to avoid the real turmoil they cause. Somehow the minor psychological pain is easier to stomach than the assorted limbs left strewn along the avenue.

For God's sake, how many times do I need to be told by a

friend of the terrorists that they were "normal"? I suppose this vindicates abnormal people like me—but interviewing the bomber's classmates about his habits is like interviewing kittens about yarn. What the hell is normal in college anyway? Smoking weed and running through the halls with your underwear on your head and your ass painted red is normal for most boys in college. What these interviewees really mean is that he didn't seem like a wild-eyed Islamic fundamentalist. But you won't get them to say that. They've got that house in the Hamptons to pay off.

Bottom line: I hate root causes. And I do not mean the big root cause that every cool gasbag ignores (Islamic supremacy). I mean the root cause baloney like, "Was little Billy not fitting in?" As Melissa Harris-Perry stated on MSNBC, the fact that the two bombers were Muslim wasn't that important to the case. Really? Then what is important? Their hobbies? Their Netflix queue? Maybe it's the jock mentality that led them to make these choices, right? Maybe if they boxed less, and hugged more, we'd all be safer!

She's wrong, of course. The fact that they were inspired by radical Islam is relevant to the legal case. That's why the little shitbag terrorist faces terrorism, not murder, charges. It goes back to his motive. He and his brother followed Sheik Feiz Mohammed, an Australian Muslim supremacist who posts videos advocating death and rape and loads of other good stuff. Since 2001, there have been 104 criminal cases of domestic jihadism. I'm thinking that this is a pattern even a left-wing automaton like Harris-Perry might find. But if she did, she'd probably be fired by MSNBC. She makes Katy seem like the smart Perry.

On the day following the arrests, the *New York Times* devoted at least five pages to the event, with maybe one sentence on the terrorists' Muslim ties—pertaining to how the FBI had previously investigated the older brother. Oddly, they gave about the same amount of coverage to the diversity of restaurants in the Boston area. As my friend Gavin pointed out, "it felt like the writer had a gun to his head when he brought up the ties to terror." You can feel air thick with secular prayer—the media wanted so badly for this to be anything but Muslim supremacists that now they're suffering from a truth hangover. All this truth has given them a headache. They were little kids on Christmas morning who didn't get the present they were dying for. Sorry MSNBC—better luck next terror bombing.

The preoccupation with psychological motives that spur a killer does nothing but benefit the killer, while energizing other losers to do the same thing to achieve attention and immortality. (It also drowns out the compassion necessary for the fiend's victims.) Now people will wonder if it's not the monster's fault but ours because we didn't help it fit in. That can only create more monsters.

The root-cause theory can be destroyed in one simple sentence: "A lot of people don't fit in and don't blow people up."

We've all had bad things happen in our lives. Life is hard for everyone, but we all don't wage jihad as a response. If all of us have similar problems, then a killer having them too is meaningless. The surviving scumbag kid was impressionable? Aren't we all? In the 1970s I wore tight white flares and walked like John Travolta. Later I went punk. Then there was the lambada period. We're all as impressionable as pizza dough.

We now spend days obsessing over the killer's personal life—and why? What's with the interest in evil? It's because "cool" made it so. It's no longer necessary to follow any structural norm to be respected or envied. As long as you do something huge, with enormous worldwide impact, you will have an audience's attention. And the audience now seeks to know "why"—because the explanation has to be more than "they're evil." We love to dig deep into the psyche instead of accepting the simplicity and banality of evil.

The result is that we spend less time trying to stop evil and more time trying to understand it. And that enhances and encourages the "evil" personality. Even more, over time we tend to like them—glamorize them, even. We become the Clarice to their Hannibal. The Harry Morgan to Dexter Morgan. Dana Perino to her dog. Celebrities buy art made by serial killers. Rock stars move into homes where gruesome crimes unfolded. Aging actors make celluloid valentines for hippie terrorists. All of this is connected to the cool embrace of darkness. Modern pop culture has trained us to gravitate toward the guilty instead of their victims. The media has turned us all into naive defense attorneys. Johnnie Cochran wasn't the truly cool one. The female prosecutor and her black assistant were. Quick, can you name them? Of course not.* They didn't get the endless media accolades. And they didn't get the conviction, either, for similar reasons. They were on the uncool side of the case.

The media's obsession with a killer's emotional depth (of which there usually is none) inevitably makes them more appealing. What if we had just decided to stop covering the bombers once the arrest was made? What if we made a pact not to discuss their backgrounds and stopped showing their damn pictures? What if we stopped making it advantageous to the angry and lonely to do horrible things? What if I stopped asking questions?

Here is my prediction for the future of the surviving Boston Bomber. He'll get life in prison. He'll get married (after choosing

---

*Marcia Clark and Chris Darden.

from a number of proposals). He'll get fans. He'll get a PhD. He'll get published (poetry, my guess). He'll get famous friends (who'll claim he's innocent). He'll get laid. In short he'll have a richer life than most people who didn't bomb the limbs off Americans. And he'll have famous admirers to thank for all of it.

Take Amanda Palmer, apparently a singer no one has really heard of for a while, who wrote an actual, *dreadful* love poem to the surviving terrorist. Instead of writing a poem for the victim, she chose the killer as her muse. Perhaps, in her head, she'll be that one crazy lady who marries him—because she sees his good side!

Here is a sampling of her horrible nonrhyming mess, entitled "a poem for dzhokhar," published on April 21, 2013:

> *You don't know how orgasmic the act of taking in a lungful*
> *of oxygen is until they hold your head under the water.*
> *You don't know how precious your iPhone battery time was*
> *until you're hiding in the bottom of the boat.*

Yes, she really is empathizing with a terrorist's need for his iPhone. She is empathizing with his fear of waterboarding. She is also empathizing with his orgasms, I guess. She is empathizing with a creep who just blew up a child. She is without question beyond pond scum. (If there were a planet full of pond scum, the pond scum who lived there would refer to her as "lower than us.")

So what is her message here? Well, that terror really is a lifestyle choice. It's like taking up lacrosse or joining a frat. Or becoming a cool singer with ego-driven opinions disguised as thoughtfulness. If you'd only put yourself in *their* shoes, you'd understand, says the cool singer. However, Palmer doesn't put herself in the shoes of the victims, because they were blown off.

What I hate most: How the cool pretend to be so smart

when they contemplate the root causes of bad men. They act like what they're doing is somehow educational—even helpful or, most laughably, thoughtful. It's none of that. Instead it's pure selfishness—mental masturbation, in front of a crowd—an act of self-pleasure masquerading as analysis. In a way, they make the whole mess a lot worse because they dilute the comprehension and condemnation of horror. They turn evil into a therapy session. Instead of taking his life, now we offer the murderer a new one. Explain root causes to their families, please.

My helpful tip when someone brings up root causes: Remind them of that youthful bomber laying his deadly contraption right behind that young boy. Or the fact that the scum shot the MIT police officer Sean Collier in the back of the head.

Mindless root-causers cannot handle the contemplation of those deeds, however. They refuse to ponder the actual deeds: to look at evil in its face instead of rooting through the killer's background for "signs" that he might have been bullied. The more they ask "why," the more they avoid "how" and "who."

People seem shocked that one of the bombers actually went to a party after the bombing. And to the gym! Oh, *why* would he do that! Oh my, the bomber was on Twitter! *Why* would he go there? Stop asking why, for God's sake.

Evil people do work out and go to parties. It's what makes them evil. They don't care. Remember, it's not like they did anything majestic. All they proved is that it's very easy to leave primitive bombs among innocents and run. That's all it takes for cowards.

But isn't that what being cool is all about? The ability to subvert society and throw existing structures into chaos? Walking into a crowd and fucking shit up? Don't those lowlifes who wish to leave a horrific impact really wish to be cool? The wake of destruction behind them is so awesome! This is where godless self-involvement and Muslim supremacy meet: a desire to die big, to be remembered.

That may be the ultimate consequence of cool: that a life of obscurity is viewed as somehow inferior to a life of infamy. Being a good person who lives quietly but valiantly on a pretty ruthless planet, but manages to find grace in everyday things, no longer means much. Better to scatter your hate into a thousand bloody pieces. And have idiots write a poem about it.

PURE IDIOCY

How has cool destroyed the pride one takes in work? Look around you. Pop culture, through music, television, and magazines, defines the "go-getter" as a clueless clone working for the man. From the first time you had to read *Death of a Salesman*, you were told that working nine to five was for suckers. (One wonders if it would have been so revered if it had been called *Death of a Performance Artist Named Chloe* or *Death of a Homeless Junkie Named Gentle Ben*.) I'm pretty sure that when the play was written, millions of people around the world would have died for that job and lifestyle. And did.

When I worked at Rodale, the publishing company that puts out magazines like *Prevention* and *Men's Health*, the place seemed sincere in its mission. Which was to make lots of money while appearing not to be interested in making lots of money. Instead, it claimed to be interested in promoting "natural," "organic," and "pure." (As in "pure profit." Which I salute.)

There was also the magazine *Organic Farming*, which sadly had no centerfold. It later morphed into something called *Organic*

Style, which folded after becoming an "organic ATM." This is no surprise in an arena (publishing) where losing money is an Olympic event. Also, the name *Organic Style* just sounds gross. I hear it, and I think of hair gel made of pig compost. It was no surprise to me that the publisher of such dreck, Maria Rodale, published an "open letter" to President Obama on the *Huffington Post* proclaiming that the gassing of Syrians with chemical weapons was no different from Americans using pesticides on their produce. We're all Hitlers, it seems. You cannot create this idiocy in a lab, folks. It can only occur naturally.

Rodale reflected the ideology that natural is cool and manmade is evil. In the offices, you couldn't swing a cat full of hemp without hitting a person on some macrobiotic diet or a weird regimen of shrubs and herbs. One of my first friends, "Ryan" (not his real name—he might still be alive and want to offer me a cleansing), was a handsome lad in his late thirties who could have been the town playboy if his skin hadn't been dyed completely orange because of his obsessive eating of carrots and other beta-carotene products. He was a walking Creamsicle. He ran two or three times every day, never mind the weather. I would see him jogging on Lehigh Street wearing three or four layers of clothing—in the summer. He was the first manorexic I ever met, and, being orange and covered in layers, he resembled a homeless sherbet.

His lifestyle was odd but wholly defensible because it was cool. You could do anything nutty, as long as the earth didn't get hurt and what you did to yourself was somehow "natural." These were the folks who overdosed on fiber, lecturing you on climate change while passing gas that could power three tractors. (Never jog behind an organic/fitness freak. Talk about methane combustion. Who knew you could drown from flatulence?)

I get the whole thing. The earth is cool. If you like the earth, then you're cool.

And you make yourself feel cool by embracing this cool relationship. So go ahead, hug an earthquake. What do I care?

What was uncool to planet-pleasers? People like you and me with a "dependent" relationship on the planet, who use this precious orb for their own personal desires. People like corporate lawyers, doctors, accountants, housewives, cops. Just about anyone in a uniform or a suit and a tie was evil because they abused the planet daily. The only organic garden they cultivated was in their shower drain. If you didn't understand how far superior it was to mountain-bike in really expensive clothes and munch on organic buckwheat flapjacks with artisanal pomegranate syrup instead of scrambled eggs, then you weren't *one of us.*

And that's the essence of organic cool, really: exclusion. The organic health movement really is about excluding you and saying, "I am better than you because I care." And can afford to care. The cool are united by their hidden bank accounts and the rhythmic regularity of their colons.

Which is why I must make a very simple point: These people are not just uncool, they are dupes. They are wrong. Nearly all of their hobbies and amusements cost way more than what a typical Joe Schmo takes part in. Their super-cool globe-hugging lifestyle actually puts more into our capitalistic society than I ever did. They're rabid consumers in Luddite disguise and their clothing costs more than the crap I would buy on sale at the outlets in Reading, Pennsylvania.

And their philosophy is a joke too. The earth isn't benevolent. And it's far from cool. I could list all the ways that natural things kill you, but that book would be thicker than the health care bill, which is also deadly. Instead, I'll just bring up one.

When I left Rodale, my next job was at *Stuff* magazine. I wrote a feature there called "A Leper Walks into a Bar," which is, funnily enough, about a leper named José. José got leprosy when he was a teen, playing football. He got cleated on the field, and the soil there had entered his body. The soil contained armadillo feces, which spread leprosy. (Good to know this now, right?)

So, in short: My pal got leprosy from an armadillo, one of God's great creatures, a natural beast that roams this adorable planet. He did not get leprosy from a Twinkie, a Camel cigarette, or a gallon of gas. He got it from an armadillo's ass.

Anyway, José is fine, happily married, with kids—no thanks to the earth. To him, nature is uncool. Nature made him a leper. And man-made medicine helped him lead a normal life, with a great family and a great future. The earth screwed him, man saved him.

So where does all this obsession with nature and organic products take you? Well, if you're a celebrity, you'll invariably write a book about it, one with elitist, quirky recipes that no one can follow. (See the bizarre transformation of Gwyneth Paltrow's career into a twig-eating Martha Stewart. How did a blond Olive Oyl who looks like she lives on twenty-five calories a day get to write a cookbook? Mario Batali looks like he could use her to pick his teeth.) But for everyone else, following the organic trail makes them gullible, and vulnerable to idiotic ideas. And ultimately it can kill them (starting with their relationships first).

The only way a freakish health practice can take hold is if someone famous deems it cool. Look at the hysteria, driven by assorted Hollywood wackjobs, regarding vaccines. Once Jenny McCarthy opened her gob about an unsubstantiated link between autism and vaccines, her cool cachet went up. Previously a pinup drifting in and out of medium-profile relationships, she found her cool calling demonizing a practice that has saved the lives of millions. And because of this hysteria over a life-saving medical treatment, parents have avoided vaccinating their kids, putting them at risk for previously controlled illnesses. Here is where cool kills, but the cool never know, because their depth of research stops at googling their own names. Which leads me to a tweet I came across back in January 2013, from someone you've probably never heard of.

> its 2013 . . . fuck a flu shot!!! if you eat food that is
> alive & practice yoga you'll never need that bullshit

That was a tweet by a pretty cool cucumber who goes by the name of Gonjasufi. I bought his debut album, *A Sufi and a Killer*, maybe three years ago, and he ain't lying. He is a Sufi, I guess, and judging by this tweet, he's okay with killing.

I follow Gonjasufi not for medical advice, but because I really like his music. He's a freakish rapping wackadoodle, a human who sounds like the offspring of a frog and Larry King. He's also a yoga teacher, which rounds out his cool pedigree nicely. He'd be the main cartoon if PBS ran Saturday morning cartoons.

It's my fault, I guess, for following a freak when it comes to vaccinations, but I felt, that day in January 2013, that I had to respond. I replied to his tweet with:

> Tell that to families of those who died from the flu:
> 'Oh your kid should have done yoga.' Booooo.

Yes, pure poetry. A few minutes later, he wrote back:

> i believe in the power of raw food and sunlight,, .
> what's interesting is most of the kids that died had
> the flu shot . . . go figure. peace

I hate to break it to Gonja, but "most of the kids" did not die from flu shots, but from flus and other illness that targeted a public increasingly spooked by vaccinations. This sentiment is driven by celebrity-caused hysteria and a need for shallow nitwits to appear cool. If you remember, Jim Carrey was one of the most hysterical advocates of ditching vaccines, if only to impress his then-girlfriend, fellow anti-vaccine nutbag Jenny McCarthy. I don't believe it's a coincidence that as his film career waned, his political advocacy blossomed. He replaced one sort of trash with another. But at least his films never killed anyone. If you don't include "death by boredom."

The truth? The cool kills children. This item appeared on the website of WFTV in Orlando, Florida, in April 2013:

> Health officials said a baby died from whooping cough last week. This is the first whooping cough death the county has seen in decades. Officials said it's been at least twenty years or more since someone died of the disease. Whooping cough, also called pertussis, and other diseases are making comebacks, because so many parents are deciding not to vaccinate their kids. "It's really unfortunate. We're saddened to hear that an infant died of something like this," said Dain Weister with the Florida Department of Health in Orange County. Officials said the family chose not to vaccinate their child. Some parents are choosing not to fully vaccinate their children because they worry there is a link between the vaccinations and autism.

Maybe raising awareness isn't all it's cracked up to be. Is there a vaccine against stupid celebrities?

I've covered the vaccine mess elsewhere, and repeatedly—so enough. Instead, I want to focus on the one phrase that stuck with me from Gonjasufi: "I believe in the power of raw food and sunlight."

All that matters in the world is to believe. Never mind evidence or facts; as long as you believe, then you're admired for your passion. And in a modern world where every greenie, leftist, or prog embraces their iPads and iPods, as well as the organic food trucked in by, um, trucks—to Whole Foods—they still "believe" that man-made stuff is bad. They condemn anything with a human fingerprint on it—but only if it's a product they don't use. It's why you can hate Alcoa but not Apple.

And it's also really easy to be a hypocrite, if your actual lifestyle isn't monitored 24/7. You can prattle on all you want about carbon emissions at a restaurant because no one will see you desperately hailing a cab on the way home. No walking for you, Captain Caring. It's just too cold, and you need to get home to shove a candle in your ear.

Remember, for the cool, even stuff like "natural" disasters is far from natural. Hurricanes, after all, are the product of global warming, caused by man and his insatiable lust for SUVs (but not private jets). If we all lived a simpler life, the earth would reward us with flood-free lives. Never mind that these disasters have been part of the world since the world began—what's uncool is how we've exacerbated them. Crap, a CNN talking head even wondered if the allegedly sudden appearance of asteroids in 2013 was the fault of global warming. I really don't blame her. She's so used to hearing from her guests that man is the cause of everything bad in the world, she probably blames her ratings on global warming. But really, consider *that* logic. Blaming auto emissions for asteroids is the modern equivalent of a rain dance. I fear human sacrifice may be next. It better be organized by Nielsen ratings.

This nonsense is so backward and illogical that it's positively childlike. Celebrities can argue against man-made stuff with their mouths, yet how often are their mouths the beneficiary of man's heightened abilities to affect nature? Plastic bags: evil. Plastic surgery: good. Have you seen Daryl Hannah's face lately? Neither has she, apparently. To me it's about as natural as the international space station. I don't think vegan Pam Anderson's implants were grown in an organic vegetable garden. If man-made things are so harmful, Meg Ryan's lips alone must be responsible for at least ten dead polar bears.

Things from earth: cool. Things from man: uncool. And if you happen to work for a business that violates that mantra, you're part of the problem. You are evil. If you want to be cool in any modern setting, it is heartily encouraged to denigrate these things: cars, oil, pesticides, pharmaceuticals, clinical trials, food production, fracking, irradiation, pasteurization, profits, e-cigs, freeways, factories. That's off the top of my head (another target of denigration). Meanwhile, you can bet the person gaining cool cred from bemoaning any of the above is shopping at Whole Foods, the feel-good mecca for organauts. But without most of the stuff I just listed above, Whole Foods would not exist. That organic food didn't arrive on the store shelves via an incredibly disciplined group of storks. I've seen the semis out in front and they don't harness the power of yoga and haikus.

The polar opposite of organic foods, in the mind of the cool, is genetically modified foods. I blame the media for encouraging the hysterics. Not an article is published about these foods without reference to the overused phrase "Frankenfoods." But that word says more about the laziness of reporters who lack experience in the realm of science than it does about any flaws in the science. GM foods represent the most uncool of things to people pushing the "natural" lifestyle: man infecting natural foods with something evil, something impure and unnatural. It's like giving a cantaloupe an STD (which is entirely possible, I've come to find). Better heads than mine have elaborated on it, but without GM foods, many people would die. I know that's uncool to say, but it's true: Genetic modification helps feed people who would otherwise starve. Drought-resistant wheat wasn't made by angry ponytails in a teachers' lounge. It was created by thoughtful scientists to feed earth's expanding numbers. GM crops might in fact save Africa, if the anti-progress assholes would just get out of the way.

I always laugh at how something deemed cool in one culture is deadly in another. Take Gonjasufi's love for raw food. Think about what raw food is. It's what cavemen ate. Look how that turned out. They died. It's what countries, right now, on the present-day earth, must suffer through because they lack the technology and farming know-how to eat safely. Raw food is what you eat as a last resort. And what's more natural than salmonella and E. coli infections? Oh yeah, death.

It reminds me of those folks who condemn coal. Do they have any idea what's being burned—out of desperation—in other countries? Do they realize how many people die from the crap they burn to keep warm and how coal would save their lives? As Bjørn Lomborg (no, he never won Wimbledon) pointed out in the *Wall Street Journal*:

> Almost two million people, meanwhile, die each year inhaling smoke from inefficient and dirty fuels such as dried animal dung, crop residues and wood.

Another one million die from the effects of outdoor
air pollution.

And that's just in Detroit.

But who needs to hear that really, when you can rail against
climate change and coal in a heated hot tub in Breckenridge?
Lomborg also points out:

> According to statistics from the emergency disasters
> database, deaths caused by flooding, droughts, heat
> waves and storms—including the effects of global
> warming—now account for about one-twentieth of
> one percent of all deaths in the developing world.
> From 1990 to 2007, that averaged about 27,000
> deaths per year.

So, two million people die from lack of safe fuels to provide the
most important need (warmth). But instead, our politicians, activists, and celebrities would rather focus on something that may or
may not contribute to a five-figure death count. How come?

Again, the argument against coal is an argument against
man-made machines (even though coal is made by earth) and,
of course, America. Coal is America. You are cooler and braver
to blame America. Imagine if you actually pointed out that in a
world where only the warm survive, coal beats everything, hands
down. Shit, people are actually burning shit to survive. If dung
actually were an effective fuel, MSNBC could heat the entire
solar system.

Remember unpasteurized Odwalla? You can't miss their cute
little bottles of organic juices at your local deli or grocery. Crap,
sometimes my wife will even buy one (which I instantly hide

behind the rum). In 1996, the hippie-dippie company was held criminally responsible for poisoning—yes poisoning—a couple of dozen people, and killing a kid, with its apple juice. See, the juice wasn't pasteurized and therefore carried the pathogen E. coli O157:H7. That's a fancy name for a poison that destroys the cells in your intestine. It can cause diarrhea, but it can also kill you. In my mind, that's kind of uncool. The juice wasn't pasteurized so it would be seen as "pure." And pure is cool. Deadly cool. Thankfully, Odwalla learned its lesson and embraced the evil technology that is pasteurization. That's good. My wife loves the stuff, and I'd like to have her around (for a while).

Still, despite its dangers, the raw movement exists, for no other reason than it helps define the individual practicing it. Now, I'm not talking about apples and oranges, which I think most people think of when you talk about raw foods. I'm talking about idiots who think drinking unpasteurized milk makes you a better person, even if the FDA implores you not to. Maybe we should simply look at it as thinning the herd. The more people who drink raw milk, the fewer people there will be who drink raw milk. And that's got to be good for conservative candidates in an election year.

Cool folks are consumed by the idea of purity. "Are there any additives in that free-range cupcake?" "There are no pesticides involved in the making of my hemp doughnut." "Sorry, can't eat these strawberries—whoever transported them was probably listening to Rush Limbaugh in his truck." Purity is a big thing with the coolerati. But, like cool, it exists separate from the notions of good and evil. Pure sugar is delicious. What about pure cocaine? How about pure horseshit? Yep, it's 100 percent pure, but it's still horseshit.

And as with horseshit, if you use it to define your course of existence, you will die. Or you will kill others. Pure lead will kill you (it's called a bullet). Speaking of which, the EPA wants to ban lead bullets, deeming them an environmental toxin. Perhaps we can make ammunition out of tofu? The Taliban would love that!

Incidentally, if you really think organic means pure, then you're in for a helluva heartbreak. Organic farms do use pesticides and, as reported by Brian Palmer in Slate, organic wine needs eighty times more fertilizer than conventional vino. Worse, as the Consumers Union reported back in April 1998, one-quarter of organic food eaten in America was tainted with pesticides. That's a long time ago but my guess is, whatever was contaminated was probably better for you than anything else. I'm thinking, in this case, it's probably a good thing when the rules of organic food prep are violated. Some people would not be reading this sentence now if fifteen years ago pesticides weren't being used on the sly. They'd be compost.

Because organic farmers don't use conventional methods, the only way they can produce and keep up with nonorganic is to increase their acreage. More space, I thought, was a bad thing! Aren't we running out of room, people? And let's not forget, increasing acreage for organic farming only leads to the death of more little disease-carrying critters like mice, voles, and life coaches. But as long as everything's pure, then everything is cool. And when everything is cool, everything is permissible!

It's not just about food. It's also about where the food goes. Because what's the point of eating pure food if you, yourself, are impure?

And that really is the danger of accepting an ideology that transcends the basic belief in right and wrong. Sure, you can be pure—and still be rotten to the core. In that sense, there are no additives. You're perfect. A 100 percent organic jackass! But a cool one!

THE DEADLY DO-RIGHTS

If there had to be a mascot for the cool environmentalist, it's got to be the mosquito, the purveyor of a poison called malaria. That's because, in an effort to be cool, they willfully ignore science, and data that could save millions of lives all over the world, including many poor people sweating profusely in Sub-Saharan Africa who are swatting at drones far deadlier than the ones flying over Pakistan.

There's nothing cooler than putting the planet before people. The problem with this kind of coolness is that it's wrong and often deadly. How many have died because it became cool to demonize DDT? Millions of lives were saved by that evil chemical, which killed malaria-carrying mosquitoes before the cool demonized it.

No one can escape the cool's pressure to bend you to their will. They invade your hotel room, with thoughtful little placards placed on your bedside table, guilting you into participating in their thoughtful green program by using a soggy towel. They pretend it's for the sake of the Earth. But it's really about saving on Tide. It's why I now sleep only in youth hostels under the pseudonym "Lou Dobbs."

But there's nothing cooler than an environmental trend—and proof of its coolness is its ability to transcend death. Meaning, even if the trend ends in loss of human life, it's A-OK, because it's for the deadly "greater good." A small but significant example is the ban of plastic shopping bags, to be replaced by the reusable type, which took place in San Francisco in 2012. These bags were banned for a couple of reasons: One, they make life hard for seagulls (scientifically described as "filthy, gruesome flying rats that shit on your head"—an appellation occasionally hurled at me). And they're a petroleum-based product (as you know, there's nothing more uncool than oil, even under the guise of another helpful product). But what the Bay Area found out, soon enough, is that what's helpful to the birds is none too kind to nonbirds. Specifically, the human beings who get crapped on by said birds. According to researchers at the University of Pennsylvania Law School, the sacks often end up containing potentially deadly bacteria that have killed people. According to their research: "the San Francisco County ban is associated with a 46 percent increase in deaths from food-borne illnesses. This implies an increase of 5.5 annual deaths for the county." And as I think you'll agree, even an implied death can really suck.

According to the figures, that's five and a half bodies, or more precisely, fifteen of me.

They also note, in boring language that no greenie would ever concern himself with because it involves money, statistics, and budgets: "Using standard estimates of the statistical value of life, we show that the health costs associated with the San Francisco ban swamp any budgetary savings from reduced litter."

Meaning, not only is the ban deadly, it's also economically

a big, fat, pointless wash. In scientific terms, this ban is, like, "stoop-id." Of course. Budgets and human life don't rate when up against cool cloth sacks. What's a life if you don't take home your soy milk in an old fertilizer sack? To eco-maniacs, it just feels good to be acknowledged for doing the right thing, even if the right thing is the deadly thing. It's just another element to being cool: Cloth makes you Fonzie, plastic makes you Potsie. (And paper makes you Al, but at this point the analogy breaks down.)

Which is why, when faced with facts that undermine the cool factor, the cool combat the truth with propaganda and outright lies. Take Rachel Carson's seminal (i.e., full of noxious baloney) environmental screed, *Silent Spring*, which greenies hail as their bible. Carson proves Gutfeld rule number thirty-four: If there is anything truly harmful to the environment, it's books on the environment. *Silent Spring* achieved something hardcore greenies always wanted: thinning the herd without getting blamed for it.

Carson—a biologist who had worked for the US Fish and Wildlife Service—wrote a book damning an insecticide used to wipe out bad stuff like malaria, typhus, and the bedbug. But DDT's real benefit was to kill mosquitoes, which helped put an end to malaria in many places throughout the world. But according to Carson, DDT would kill birds and cause cancer in humans. Most of the claims focused on data showing the thinning of eggshells in some feathered friends. In 1972, the Environmental Protection Agency banned the stuff, thanks to Carson's book, and most other countries fell in line. Including countries, sadly, that really needed the chemical the most (i.e., in Africa).

Look, I'm no expert in chemistry (which I suspect you knew), but I can smell exaggeration a mile away, and it was clear that Rachel had gone overboard on DDT. Yes, DDT is a poison. That's why it's great—it kills things that might *kill us*. But as for this chilling proof concerning its deadliness to humans or fowl, the evidence is strictly for the birds. No one bothered to check, however, because it wouldn't have been cool to disagree with Carson. In a cocktail party where you wish to impress people, it's easier to go off on a phony tangent about the brilliance of *Silent Spring* and the evil of "man-made chemicals." That's way cooler than saying, "You know what? DDT is good shit. There's some in this drink, in fact."

People—millions perhaps—died because one idea sounded cooler than the facts. While DDT was in use, malaria went the way of the dodo, disappearing in the United States and elsewhere. It's as extinct as Hollywood patriotism. And without DDT? Without it, malaria returned like a long-lost Baldwin brother. The World Health Organization claims up to one hundred million lives might have been saved by this evil, vicious pesticide. (That has to be the worst comeback since Marion Barry.) Some blame malaria's revival on climate change, but that's just a cool way of avoiding the truth and perpetuating more death. You retain your cool credentials by avoiding the DDT question, while amping them up by bringing another "hot button" issue into the mix. If you could only say, "Reusable cloth sacks used for shopping, by reducing our dependence on oil used to make plastic bags, will help curb carbon emissions, which in turn will reduce malaria, and will in turn save millions of lives." Yeah, it's total BS, but you sound really cool saying it. I think I deserve a Nobel Prize (I'll take Obama's) just for coming up with it.

So here are the noncool facts: Malaria infects something like millions of people a year, primarily in Africa. Up to three million die. Right now, you hear a bit about celebrities backing mosquito nets to help stop this "greenie genocide." The nets help, no doubt, but they ain't DDT. From 2000 to 2008, nets are said to have saved 250,000 babies in Sub-Saharan Africa. Quite an achievement. But only if you ignore the millions who have died since Carson's book and the DDT ban it caused. I'm glad the babies lived, but I wish there could have been more. Maybe we should be netting a few of the celebrities instead.

An itchier consequence of a world without DDT? You now have an old friend to share a new bed with: the bedbug. There's nothing more uncool than spending the night with someone you just met in a Lower East Side bar, only to wake up looking like you slept on a rack of ferrite beads. Bedbugs have been around forever (since the time of the early colonists, or when Harry Reid entered Congress) and were common pests on the old sailing ships way back when. They were pretty much everywhere, often considered the top pest, in line with cockroaches and Girl Scouts. What got rid of them? Hint: It rhymes with DDT. Because it is DDT.

The bugs disappeared in developed countries thanks to the chemical, and you'd only really find them in joints like prisons, hostels, or my office.

But now they're back. For a long while, New Yorkers were blessed with screaming headlines about bedbugs infiltrating up-scale shops and tourist meccas, including the Times Square movie houses. I made the mistake of looking up a website that tracks bedbug infestation, and then entering my zip code. Any place where bedbugs had been found and sprayed was represented by a red dot. My neighborhood was a sea of blood. I'm living in the freakin' Amazon over here. Maybe this is what the super meant when he said the building allowed animals. (I've since moved.)

I still see exterminators around town, some equipped with bug-sniffing dogs (at least that preoccupation keeps the dog from finding my drugs). The bugs infest hotels, including the nice ones where the cups aren't wrapped in plastic. The upside: I no longer have to go to movies with my wife. Something I hate and she loves. All I have to say is, "That theater just got nailed for bedbugs," and we end up drinking instead. Mention bedbugs to a woman, and they go into a skin-inspecting frenzy. Bottom line is that bedbugs are back all over the world, and it's pretty much due to one major cool achievement: the removal of DDT.

Fact is, DDT was the bouncer that kept so many undesirables at bay. But the cool, too shallow to do the research, rallied against this precious pesticide. The result—more New Yorkers are scratching, and somewhere else far away, people are dying. Not cool.

NUKING THE
NUCLEAR FAMILY

W hy do families exist? It took me forty-eight years of mistakes, idiocy, and regret to figure it out. Humans are not born with installed memories, handed over from those who spawned us. Babies do not come with ready-made software. The brat is, by nature, programmed not just to poop, but to make crappy mistakes. Hence the existence of parents, who are supposed to transmit information culled from their own awful mistakes. Moms can tell a daughter "not to give away the milk for free." As clichéd and simplistic as it sounds, everyone pretty much gets the message. My girlfriends certainly did. When Mom isn't there to talk about the cow, culture is let out to pasture, wallowing in poop. And tracking it everywhere. We all need a mom to transmit that "cow" story, more than ever.

Despite thousands of years of evidence that damns the practice, girls still fall for "cool guys." Mom and Dad exist to inform kids that that choice never ends well. Common truths are common for a reason: They're true. Bad boys are bad; beauty works temporarily, and as it fades, the bad boy trades you in for a younger model, if he doesn't die on a motorcycle on the way to pick up an ounce of weed from his ex-wife who's now a dealer. This is old news, but since this old news doesn't come preinstalled in the young, it's always going to be new to them.

The cool, through media like motion pictures and music, separate children from their best information delivery systems (parents). And when these IDSs try to reason with their newly cool-indoctrinated offspring, their attempts are met with mockery by the world at large, which also embraces the cool's attack on morality. The scenario creates a breezy nonmorality, which predictably benefits the cool, abortion clinics, and ex-wives who deal weed. A parent who tries to give advice to his child will now be portrayed as an outmoded oaf. It's why MTV won more minds than Ronald Reagan. It started with matinee idols and led to pop singers, then rock stars, then hip-hop artists with reality shows about lifestyles that contain some style, but no life. Again, see Miley Cyrus's convulsive tongue. That organ should be the mascot for an insipid, declining morality. Then quarantined. Or examined for scurvy.

I'm aware that it's hilariously uncool to point out our poisoned culture. To be considered cool, you must agree to ignore the decline or, better, celebrate it. Writers do this all the time, in sitcoms, talk shows, or monthly think pieces, reassessing what naturally should be considered a flaw in our cultural development, as something perfectly acceptable, even morally superior. Just weeks ago, a talk show host, Touré (which is French for "imbecile"), waxed poetic on MSNBC about how a girlfriend's abortion saved his life or, more important, his career. I suppose we were supposed to applaud the bravery of a man who feels he must go by one name. But I just saw a dweeb, in an effort to gain cool points, by out-feminizing the feminists. If Touré's parents had acted like Touré, we never would have been graced with his amazing monologue on the value of abortion. I doubt he's thought too much about that. Touré doesn't realize that his greatest argument for abortion is actually his own show. And does he really put an accent over the second syllable of his name? Seriously, he thought about that. How cliché.

Writers participate in this sort of high drama and inherently phony crap because it is their exercise in cool, as lame as it may be. Take Julie Drizin, who runs something impressive to people who don't know better—the Journalism Center on Children and Families at the Philip Merrill College of Journalism at the University of Maryland. (How does that fit on a diploma?) In short, you can bet that whatever she does for a living does less for children than the title does for her. In a column from 2012 in the *American Journalism Review*, she takes credit for having the word "illegitimate" removed from the AP stylebook. Apparently this word really upsets her. She describes it "like fingernails on a blackboard." (Apparently neither she, nor the *AJR*, is really bothered by clichés.) When she heard an NPR host actually use the dreaded term, she says, "it was like an electric shock through the radio that spurred me to action." She's like a bad-language Batman! She quickly e-mailed the editors of *The Associated Press Stylebook* and instructed them to drop the phrase "illegitimate child." And in their brave, judicious fashion, the AP did.

Why? Drizin explains, "Because it's patriarchal, judgmental, and out of touch with reality." And also, she'll get to write about it, and pat herself on the back. I'm sure there was a sabbatical and a journal article in it. Another major step forward for the West! My God, China must find us hilarious. Or at least illegitimate.

I mean, she wants to ban "illegitimate" but continues to use "patriarchal"? There you have it, people: another blowhard bludgeoning common sense with academic catchphrases that function like breathing on calcified campuses everywhere. When you hear the word "patriarchal," you know it's not a compliment, and it's always tied to the equally evil phrase "judgmental." Remember, in a world where dads are constantly portrayed as goofy, bumbling, and secretly abusive, pointing out the sobering truths about unmarried moms is like farting in an elevator (which has cost me at least two promotions).

But while banishing a phrase might elevate the cool factor of the director of an institute, what does it really do for actual children and families the institute is supposed to help? Do we think removing a word from a stylebook is really going to reduce illegitimacy or help families? That by removing the word, you remove the problem? (Yes, I get it—it's not really a problem! No child is illegitimate—they're all precious living creatures . . . unless they're fetuses.

Maybe we should ban the term "family." It's so oppressive!

I argue the opposite: It's dangerous to remove a word that represents a fact that these children are born out of wedlock. When you start replacing facts with feelings, you disturb the equilibrium between right and wrong, confusing them as one and the same while encouraging more destructive behavior. As a stigma is erased, a behavior becomes more prevalent. (I'd say out-of-wedlock births are the "new normal," but I hate that phrase almost as much as Julie hates "illegitimate.") As reported in the Daily Caller and elsewhere, more than 50 percent of all births to American women under thirty are out of wedlock. (Wait, is "wedlock" also a bad word? And what about percentages? Those imply math, which requires values . . . I'm so confused!) It's society as envisioned by Murphy Brown.

There is little doubt that having a child out of wedlock is not the greatest reality for the child, compared with being born to a two-parent household (still better than abortion, though). It increases the chances that the child will live a life marked by poverty, crime, and emotional problems. This is not to say you can't be poor, thuggish, or psychotic in a two-parent household; I fulfill two of those descriptors and had a decent mom/dad childhood. And of course, you can point to a few people who did okay in a "broken" home, including our own president. But that's because he had great, caring grandparents who made up for a bad dad. The point is, when you need to bring up exceptions as examples, you're on the losing side of the debate.

But we all know it's not cool to point this out. How come? Because for the white, educated folks, it's not as big a problem as it is for others. More important, even if it's a problem for minorities, you really can't say that. It's just too mean-spirited to make such claims. So while 29 percent of white kids are born to single women, the number jumps to 53 percent for Latinos and 73 percent for blacks. Bottom line: It's not cool to point out illegitimate children, even if pointing them out is meant to help these children, or rather, everyone. The removal of the word "illegitimate" from the AP stylebook isn't about the behavior, but their bigotry. It's actually bigoted on the AP's part to think certain people cannot handle the truth. Don't we want men to marry and stick around? Is it wrong to point that out? Is it racist to expect that from *everybody*?

How does cool play into the rise of the single moms? It's the cause. We've had hormones for millions of years—I certainly got my fair share—and humans are horny animals. But where we once valued scruples, now we mock them. Mercilessly.

Think about all the stuff pop culture derides. It almost entirely boils down to anything that champions delayed gratification. We've got seemingly benign sitcom characters instructing us that marriage is not a necessity for happiness (pick any episode of a chick-centric sitcom) and we've got the even cooler ones featuring teenagers banging in cemeteries or sticking their fingers up first dates' butts (both hilarious plot points in *Girls*—the most demeaning thing to happen to women since Juicy sweatpants). Married couples are portrayed as goofy and joyless; the singles are always smarter and having way more fun.

Look, I get it. I sound like Billy Graham. Or Dan Quayle (remember his criticism of *Murphy Brown*?) But maybe Quayle was right on a few things. And it's not just old white guys who see where this is headed. Black conservatives get it too, which is why they are considered the least cool group in the country, ranking just beneath Maroon 5 and the Kardashians. (Maybe we could combine those two and maroon the Kardashians for five years? Just an idea.)

With cool trumping character, men no longer find marriage as enticing as they did forty years ago. Modern women, egged on by their eager and horny male friends, forfeited the most potent power they had: their vagina. A pro-abortion meme on Twitter goes by "brochoice," and their message is simple—that limits on abortion limit their chances of having recreational sex. At least they're honest about their desires, the scamps. The fact that some women praise a theory that makes them little more than receptacles for sperm seems slightly more than sad. And to an angry feminist (redundant), that comment makes me guilty of "slut-shaming"!

I'd say sleeping around leads to feelings of illegitimacy, but I don't want to hurt anyone's feelings. But I know too many women who feel lost because they wasted a better part of their youthfulness pleasuring men who had no interest in sticking around. (I can safely say I was one of those men, and I feel pretty crummy for it. But at least I didn't leave a trail of little Gregs behind me, I hope. One little Greg is enough.)

As the pool of husbands and dads disappears, the government gets bigger in order to play that role. There is a connection between our willingness to sacrifice our scruples and the government's willingness to step into our lives. Hence the 2012 campaign creation of "Julia" during President Obama's reelection campaign. The Web campaign meant to show how the government will be there through every important step in a woman's life—from school, to health, to work, to death. Instead it reminded me of how phony the cool independence of the aging single woman really is. They just exchanged one husband (a real, live, breathing one) for another (a government program).

But as the composite young woman, Julia is exalted by the cool, and the fantasy of a traditional life is ridiculed. Everywhere. Or more specifically, in Warwick, Rhode Island, where a mural in a high school had deeply angered . . . someone.

Talk about uncool. The painting was supposed to depict a man's life, from youth to adulthood, ending with him standing with a woman and child, with a pair of wedding rings above their heads. I know—I can only imagine what's next—a grown man and a boy playing catch? Why does it have to be "catch"? And why is the boy in pants? This rigid patriarchal dictatorship of gender roles has got to stop! Where is Julie Drizin?

The mural was being painted at Pilgrim High (which sounds like something you get from smoking corn husks), by a young artist named Liz Bierenday. No surprise—she was told by the vice principal that someone had complained about the offensive content. Apparently the mural didn't reflect the "life experiences" of every single student there. According to the artist, she didn't mean to offend anyone. "I didn't mean to offend anyone," she said (see, I wasn't lying there, was I?). She then explained that she was painting how she thought life would unfold. "Like after college you get a job and settle down." She also said, "Like, I feel bad."

I would too if I kept using the word "like" as punctuation. But, like, I'm on her side.

She actually was guiltier of a greater sin: She saw life the way her parents or grandparents saw it. It's a prism that is so uncool these days, it's comical. This young woman felt getting married and having kids and all the stuff that comes with it sounded kinda nice. You know, the way 99 percent of human civilization always has (except the French). Jesus, where the hell has she been the last twenty years? Settling down is for *losers*. You're basically admitting you don't have the guts to be your own person. Marriage means you're just a half of a thing, when you can be a whole thing. A whole angry thing that hates other things!

The end result: The part of the mural featuring the wedding rings was painted over. But then a school superintendent insisted she finish the mural as she had planned. Which is a happy ending, if you like happy endings.

Truth is, these days "happy endings" means something else (ask Beckel) and living "happily ever after" is a fantasy for the uncool and stupid. You've got to be naive and irrelevant to buy into the appeal of a stable family environment—or believe that it might be a tad superior to its competing lifestyle. I bet you couldn't get a feminist to admit a married-with-children life beats being a coprophilic activist sex worker who makes her own hours; the former gave up on her dreams to submit to a husband, and the latter is expressing her freedom from the normative views of traditional lifestyles! You go . . . coprophilic activist sex worker! You raise awareness with every orgasm!

So why are families uncool? Well, it's cool to rebel against your family when you're growing up. But you're supposed to get over that, at some point. It's called becoming an adult. Sure, you can hate Mom and Dad for a little bit (one year, maybe two, tops), and you usually return to the fold after admitting that they were right most of the time. But these days, a stable family is seen as uncool because extolling the virtues of such a unit excludes those who don't live that way. And that is hurtful. And being hurtful is uncool. Would anyone have questioned the mural if it had been two gay centaurs copulating on a rainbow? (Probably not, and that would be great, since I've spent the last four months painting one in my basement. It's been a struggle getting it right, but when it's done, it'll be worth all the money spent on nude escorts I used as models.)

Fact is, this student's mural is about the most rebellious thing you've never heard of, and this girl, in my mind, is a modern-day Dennis Hopper on a Harley. Her thinking is against the predictable grain of the modern progressive. Is it wrong to say that one way of living is superior to another? Not that she was saying that, but so what if she was? People who live in a traditional family structure tend to do better in life. Although I am sure there are people who believe, after reading this story, that the poor girl needs to be deprogrammed, for it's just untenable that, in this age, she would have such weird, uncool thoughts about "sex and gender roles." She was probably abused! By her evil white dad! Who listens to Mark Levin! There must be some repressed memories of Satanic rituals in there somewhere!

In a nation governed by hurt feelings, it's clear that this heathen simply doesn't care about all the people different from herself. Should romantic novels be banned because lonely people out there might find them insensitive to their plight? Who do you think reads them? Lonely people! What about sports? Should they be curtailed because they marginalize the uncoordinated? It's one reason I never watch lacrosse. (There are many others.)

Never mind that when the public is presented with alternative views and lifestyles unlike those of the majority, the feelings of the majority are never considered. Empathy is only a one-way street.

Remember the elephant-dung-encrusted image of the Virgin Mary that was once brought to the Brooklyn Museum? (Which says more about Brooklyn than religion, incidentally.) No one asked me how I felt about it. In fact I don't think anyone really gave a damn about the "feelings" of Christians, since movies and television have informed the world that we don't have feelings. Instead, Christ-lovers just have prejudices, bad hair, and closeted feelings for the same sex.

In this country, a mural of two wedding rings is uncool, while a Virgin Mary made of dung is cool. What BS. Head to head, the marriage mural beats the dung art hands down, for it dares to say something modern art would never have the guts to say—that an innate desire for a traditional life isn't so bad. And that delayed gratification beats immediate satisfaction, hands down. It's healthier and more stable, and, oddly enough, offers you the freedom to do things you couldn't do if your life were an unstable, angry pile of dung. As the king of the uncool, Ronald Reagan, once said, "Work and family are at the center of our lives, the foundation of our dignity as a free people." Translated by me: You can't be a freak without first having a foundation. (I think that's what he meant.)

That message never bubbles up in the art world because it's so uncool. And what passes for daring in art is really conformity. Conformity of the worst kind, in fact—censorship.

Which leads me to my solution to this mess—if you want

a traditional nuclear family to survive, what do you do? Perhaps it's time to champion *that* as an alternative lifestyle. Make it sound rebellious and different. Because in reality, that's what it's become. It's also tougher, by the way. Responsibility always is. But it's just too Fred MacMurray for the progressive journals and the sad sacks who pretend to read them.

Treating family like an extreme sport may be the only way the cool might be tricked into thinking it's a good thing. And before they know it, they'll be mowing lawns, working sixty-hour weeks, and screaming at their kids to turn down the music. They will have turned into their parents, which is probably the coolest thing that could happen to them, ever.

Which leads me to another question. How uncool is it to be a married dad? Really uncool. How about a married mom? Super uncool.

Remember during the election when a Democratic strategist, Hilary Rosen, went after Mitt Romney's wife, Ann? It was on CNN back in April 2012, when Rosen said that Romney had "never worked a day in her life." Mind you, Ann had raised five sons—and if that's not work, Rosen's never seen a hamper full of men's underwear. It qualifies as a Superfund site.

Because it was an election season, her attack on Ann got a lot of media attention, and Rosen quickly vanished from the scene in order to prevent further harm to her guy, President Obama. (The community organizer and no-show senator.) After all, her next trick might be criticizing the comatose for being lazy. Amazing that this lady is a PR expert. Judging from this screwup, it's likely it was she who's never worked a day in her life. It's unlikely she ever worked a day outside of government, that's for sure.

But forget the politics. The point of this screwup: It could only have occurred if Hilary felt everyone agreed with her. She's grown up with, been schooled with, gone to cocktail parties with people who agree with her. The lesson inculcated at every opportunity: The chick who works is cool. What's uncool: The chick with kids who stays home to take care of them. *Come on, America,* Hilary was saying, *you're with me on this one! Being a mom—and nothing else—is really nothing at all.*

I bet a stay-at-home mom would know how to clean up this mess better than Rosen. But don't be angry at Rosen, for it's always refreshing when a progressive reveals itself to the world by saying something they all really believe to be true. It's like watching a rare animal outside its comfy habitat acting like a rare animal. You might not see it again, acting this way in public. For what you heard is what the cool people say in the parties that neither you nor I attend. This is how the cool really feel: that Ann Romney is an example of the quaint, inferior, and irrelevant prefeminist gal. She's a joke. A dinosaur in Anne Klein pantsuits. An arcane caricature, like the secretary in *Beetle Bailey.* She's not really a real woman by modern standards. No, she's just a nonentity whose lifestyle choices clearly were not her own. She couldn't seriously *want* to raise a beautiful family, while married to a loving husband, and look forward to the two of them growing old together. Why do that, when you can be a talking head and mock it all on CNN? You'll get car service to and from work!

From the cool perspective, a full-time, stay-at-home mom (what we used to call, simply, "mom") is completely blind to her own hopelessness, a victim of false consciousness and every other fifty-dollar word you learned in grad school from wispy weirdos in granny glasses. This is why the media embraced Sandra Fluke (pronounced "Flook," no matter what she says) over Ann Romney. Fearlessly fighting for free crap is cool, but raising kids? Uncool.

And the end result from this perspective: a message to girls that desiring a full life is impossible, unless you divorce yourself from things that might in fact make you happy. The stay-at-home mom—perhaps the most influential, powerful force for our nation's future—is suddenly not a guardian of our most important resource. She's a fascist prison guard, wielding a bloody wooden spoon (which would make a good movie, actually).

This all came about because Ann Romney had talked to her husband about the state of the economy, and he actually listened to her. And that's what Rosen objected to—how can you listen to a mom about the economy? I guess she doesn't realize it's the moms who do most of the purchasing in a home and keep track of the bills. But something tells me Hilary has someone do that for her, since she considers herself an "expert" at more important things. Basically Rosen just said, "Ann should just shut up and cook. Get a graduate degree and a fully loaded Prius, and we'll talk."

This is poison, for it creates a new kind of peer pressure. Whereas before we were encouraged to marry and start families, now we have our most "successful" voices championing the opposite—or rather denigrating a basic, tried-and-true method of survival. Families work. Having a mom and dad is a pretty good thing, worth painting about. Thinking about starting a family of your own is not a bad idea. Sure, it's about as cool as argyle socks, but argyle socks can be pretty cool and you want to be stylish. One thing I learned—you're supposed to wear them on your *feet*. Who knew?

THE GUILTY PARTIES

What happened to Wisconsin? Seriously, *what happened to Wisconsin*? It used to be a fun place, most notably home to the Troll Capital of the World, where I'm considered above average height.

But it's also home to the new, Caucasian bigot. I'm not referring to the stereotypical white racist you see in your basic cable movie. Not skinheads with swastika tattoos on their testicles and etchings of Hitler hanging in their trailer. Instead the Wisconsin variety are whites who charge that all whites are racist, while claiming to defend People of Color. Their radical agenda isn't about healing; it's about breaking up and breaking apart. It's about preventing a color-blind society from forming, and replacing it with warring factions divided by skin pigment.

To start with, the University of Wisconsin–Superior (superior to what? an online kindergarten?) launched the "Unfair Campaign" in 2012 to boost the "public awareness" about the widespread problem of racial privilege. Their marketing shtick: writing words like "unfair" on white students' faces. They also Magic-

Markered on their own nonsensical noggins a plethora of grievances against white people, as experienced by People of Color. As you can imagine, their faces look like a road map of victimization, a paean to pain. According to the website Mediaite, the university released a statement defending this exercise, claiming it was "designed to be very provocative."

Ah yes . . . "provocative"! Whenever something really stupid is performed in an effort to score cool points, it's described as "provocative." In commonsense language, it translates into "annoying." And "pointless." And "academic." And usually "harmful." It's important to note that this campaign wasn't the university's idea alone. It was launched as a group effort by a collection of community sponsors. Meaning, people who think community organizing is a real vocation.

The Wisconsin Department of Public Instruction (or WDPI for you initialism fans) conducted their own separate effort to expose white privilege, suggesting that some of their white workers "wear a white wristband as a reminder about your privilege." And by privilege, they mean the many advantages white people have over all People of Color. We are now at a time when being born white is a fundamentally racist act. If you are white, just by procreating, your parents committed, or rather produced, a hate crime. You are a hate baby (a "hateby," for short). You should be ashamed of yourself. I bet even the diapers you wore were white. From now on, all of my Depends will be black. They already are (I sat in something).

The WDPI has a Web page explaining their thoughts on white privilege. This is where members of VISTA (Volunteers in Service to America, or HEAY*) can take tests and read other

_____
*Had enough acronyms yet?

stuff for the purposes of further guilt-building. The sad part: These VISTA workers are supposed to help the poor. Instead they're annoying them. Because it's way cooler to expound on your own white privilege than look up ways to apply for building permits if some poor guy wants to open a laundromat (which is racist, if your intent is to make your whites "whiter"). Seriously, can you imagine if you actually needed real employment information from these banal bureaucrats? You'd be better off waiting for Obama's next "pivot to jobs." (We're on #7. He pivots enough to join the Bolshoi.)

This stuff would be laughable if it weren't being lauded in academic circles (otherwise known as circle jerks) and harming poor people in Wisconsin.

Check out the department's website, which offered suggestions for the privileged to help facilitate their desire for white penance. For example:

- Set aside sections of the day to critically examine how privilege is working
- Put a note on your mirror or computer screen as a reminder to think about privilege
- Make a daily list of the ways privilege played out and steps taken or not taken to address privilege
- Find a person of color who is willing to hold you accountable for addressing privilege

(All of which could be shorthanded as "Vote Obama.")

I love that last part. Your mission: Find someone to condemn you. Why not save time—get married.

This, my friends, is what passes for organized religion to-day—at least for people who find paganism too much of a commitment. Instead of confession, you kneel before the Perceived Aggrieved—and take your punishment, willingly, all the while writhing in the pleasures of patronization. American universities have finally become caricatures of themselves.

Does this help the true victims of racism? Of course it doesn't, but you knew the answer to that question before I asked because you're not a moron (by definition, since you're reading my book—or having someone read it to you). All this putrid exercise in white superiority does is foster a victim's mentality and a teeming class resentment that's only meant to end up in one place: societal upheaval, full of rage and ruin, and voting "progressive." All of that stuff, for a cool racist, is pretty cool. The cool racist loves riots, after all. To them, it's not looting—it's redistribution. A race riot is actually something like a constitutional convention. Tea Party rally? Evil. Smashing the windows of local businesses in your own neighborhood? Justice! It's actually cathartic. To these tools, a race riot is just a messy yoga class.

Fact is, the cool racist really doesn't care about POC. (Now they've got me using acronyms.) The moment People of Color stop thinking about color, the cool racist loses clout. And their radical agenda is dead—which is why they must perpetuate the hate. (By the way, can we retire the word "radical" once and for all when referring to crap left-wingers come up with? Radical implies revolutionary thinking that's genuinely new. However, none of this is new; it's just applied differently by different dimwits.)

And I should remind you that the Wisconsin Department of Public Instruction is a state agency, so essentially it's the citizen who's paying for this bigotry. This new program seems to be performed under the guise of providing education for poor families, which could explain why these families are doing so poorly. If anything, having these weirdos spread these pernicious ideas to these struggling families should be labeled a hate crime, and these new racists should be hung in the town squares (by their toes, of course—I'm a tickler, not a killer).

Perhaps a better message to send People of Color is to simply point to the White House. Instead of saying "Sorry we're white," say, "A black man lives there. Well, half-black—but you get the idea." The point is, the United States is run by a black guy, and that's cool, right? For blacks, it's kinda inspirational, no? It's far more inspirational than repeatedly pointing out that we are all really sorry your ancestors were slaves fifteen decades ago. I'd love a black leader to emerge from somewhere, with a new campaign, called, "Get Over It." And that "it" could mean annoying white and black activists who rely on past oppression to guarantee their future income. Sure, slavery was an abomination. An abomination only compounded by whites who continue to live off it. They're ghouls, misery junkies. I'd boycott Wisconsin, but I rarely make it there anyway. (Something always seems to get in the way. My fear of cheese, mainly.)

THE WAR ON WARRIORS

W ho are the closest entities we have to actual superheroes in America? Aside from 3:00 a.m. talk show hosts, it's our military. They are as cool as cool can get. But ever since the 1960s the military has been regularly portrayed in the media, on campuses, and elsewhere as ultimately uncool. Before the sixties, joining the military was about sacrifice (which was sincerely cool). Now, the cool sees recruits as blind, ignorant to the realization that they're just a sap out of options.

Even a veteran like John Kerry echoes this crud. Remember what he said back in 2006?

> You know, education, if you make the most of it,
> if you study hard and you do your homework, and
> you make an effort to be smart, uh, you, you can do
> well. If you don't, you get stuck in Iraq.

Or in Congress, apparently.

To Kerry, a new recruit is sure to become just another idiot stuck in some weird-ass country, doing pointless crap for no good reason. It would be so much better if you joined another part of the government, where you could get paid to do nothing, get a sweet pension, and be a slave to comfort. (Or you could just marry the heir to a condiment fortune! He should rename his yacht *Thank You, Ketchup*.) I don't know if Kerry, an experienced warrior himself, meant to denigrate the military, but he denigrated the mind-set that would drive you to join the military. He could not believe that someone would make that choice because they saw it as an amazing opportunity. He thinks they must have thought it was the only option they had once they realized they had nothing left. What a condescending way to look at millions of really brave people. And what a simplistic mind-set from one of our leaders. Who, as I write this sentence, is pleading for an attack on Syria.

Kerry places education as a polar opposite to the military. Our current secretary of state has embraced the falsehood that education in a classroom is somehow superior to the education you gain in the military or on the battlefield. I can tell you this: I learned almost *nothing* at college that didn't involve alcohol poisoning. But I wonder, after working with veterans in various capacities over the last twenty-five years, if I would have been better off enlisting and actually learning something real about the world (and more important, myself). There's the possibility I would have been rejected (I have flat feet and a vestigial tail), and I'll never know what I'd be like in war. (I could have been a hero, or deserter, in a burka.) That's something I regret. (And it's easy to regret, now, safely, at forty-eight.) As for education, I can't possibly think of a single thing from my college years that helped me get to where I am today. I was a drunken, stupid embarrassment and, in fact, that was my major *and* minor. (Not much has changed.) I should have majored in being a major.

Back in December 2011 I came across a bizarre *Washington Post* piece on the Eisenhower Memorial, a sculpture designed by Frank Gehry. The article, a review by Philip Kennicott, was titled "Frank Gehry's Eisenhower Memorial Reinvigorates the Genre." I have not seen the memorial, but my commentary is more about the commentary than about the work of art. Yep, I'm doing a commentary on a commentary. When this book comes out, I'll do a commentary on this commentary, on that commentary . . . too.

The article reveals that the sculpture is really more about the artist than about a great warrior who became president. According to the reviewer, the success of the work was how it "inverts several of the sacred hierarchies of the classical memorial, emphasizing ideas of domesticity and interiority rather than masculine power and external display." Yeesh. That's like a car accident involving two thesauruses. Is "interiority" even a word? Did the alphabet have diarrhea?

You see where this is going. Masculine power gets the short end of the stick, which is not surprising in the modern era when sticks are always getting shortened and androgyny is cool. These days any semblance of manhood is considered masked bullying that must be undone through a relentless "It Gets Better" campaign. It's scary that even in the realm of war masculinity must be removed. I mean, you'd think war is where raw masculinity is necessary—and where it is focused and honed into awesome brute force. This is not the stuff of group hugs and "you fall and I will catch you" exercises you find at IRS retreats. If brute force is frowned upon in the military, we are all dead. In war, brute force is sort of the point, isn't it?

Thank God for Gehry, "an architect of flamboyant gestures," that he could honor a two-term president and one of America's greatest heroes through the cool, contemporary art of feminization. It's really a shame Dwight wasn't around to experience the hip metrosexuality. And to learn he embodied "interiority."

This is how the *Washington Post* describes Gehry's accomplishment:

> He has "re-gendered" the vocabulary of memorialization, giving it new life and vitality just at the moment when the old, exhausted "masculine" memorial threatened to make the entire project of remembering great people in the public square seem obsolete. If there are *murmurings within the Eisenhower family* and among Gehry skeptics and conservative critics, they probably have a lot to do with the basic feminization of the memorial language.

Uh yeah, you're right, champ. The memorial is about feminizing Eisenhower and obliterating the bravery of battle. It's about replacing fearlessness with feelings, bravery with therapy. If Dwight were alive today, he would either kill himself in disgust or try out for *Hairspray* (an evolution in sensitivity that I'm sure would've carried the day at Normandy).

The real bummer is that heroism is somehow viewed as a negative masculine behavior and that feminization is viewed as the remedy. This goes hand in hand with the view of the military by academics and media types: that the values that make a military man a military man are no longer necessary. And never were. Never mind that it's this old-fashioned morality and hardass character that ensured our survival. They aren't cool. The world has changed, and so have we. And so, one must go back in time, through memorialization, to change society's memory of those war heroes, stripping them of the core manliness that helped make them great. It's why the left can't stand Allen West. He embodies precisely the kind of manhood that scares the crap out of them. He's never joining *Hairspray*. Which is why, if he's not elected president by 2040, I'm moving to Venus. Or at least to the bunker I constructed under my bed.

Kennicott describes the work of art:

> A statue of the young Eisenhower will be placed so as to appear to be reading the events of his life to come. Eisenhower the man of action will be complemented by a more contemplative figure, a reference to the dreaminess of youth and the traditionally feminine passivity of reading.

Heck, why not just have Eisenhower in a dress picking daisies?

Kennicott goes on to describe using outdoor tapestries, which he says "subverts the idea of indoors and out, domestic and public, eliding boundaries between feminine and masculine space." Wow. "Eliding." How could this statue *not* be great?

Do you think a sculptor would ever downplay an enemy's masculinity? Do you think they'd ever consider a thoughtful piece on the feminine charms of bin Laden? No, because our enemies' manhood does not trouble them the way ours does. Ever notice how Che Guevara is portrayed? Manly.

Coolness is about subverting things that work, like our military. While subversion pulls the rug out from under goodness, no one really depends on the subverter for anything substantial. We depend on men to fight wars. We don't really depend on those who interpret warriors' masculinity for anything nearly as meaningful. While the warriors make the average citizen safer, the cool subverter just entertains grad students with disdain masked as cleverness. It's his stand-up routine, minus the jokes. In times of crisis, the subverter is the one cowering in the corner, hoarding crackers and wet wipes.

In my secret fantasies I always want to apply the idea of "subversion" to the lives of those who champion said subversion. Like, wouldn't it be great to "subvert" the artist's morning commute to work by stealing his bicycle? Wouldn't it be awesome to "subvert" his breakfast with Ex-Lax? How about "subverting" his marriage by banging his wife? Nope, for them subversion only applies to other people's traditional practices and desires. Subvert a subverter and you can bet they will collapse like a house of tarot cards. I've seen it happen—challenge an "open-minded" type with a really, *really* outrageous suggestion, and they suddenly experience a change of heart. "No, I don't want my teenage daughters to go hot-tubbing with you." Really? Oh, evolve! And bring us a six-pack of Zima. (They still make Zima, right?)

It makes you wonder what an Obama statue will be like in sixty years. Will anyone have the guts to subvert his "achievements"? Does his masculinity require a feminized makeover? Will he be shown brooding in a sarong, sneaking a joint in the backyard? Will they avoid the bin Laden killing, in favor of him doing something more humanizing, like body surfing? He played a lot of golf; they could have fun with that. Replace the clubs with long-stem roses. "The flowers represent tolerance and social justice, married to the feminization of golf, a previously masculine affair populated by white racists." That was pretty easy, and I wrote it while delousing my pet tapir.

To some, if I say our society has become more emasculated, that is seen as progress. Or cool. But it took blood and guts to get where we are, not self-esteem courses, crying circles, and hot yoga. And yes, you can find yoga in the military (it's great for your back, apparently). Fact is, all of this points to one sad and scary thing: What was once considered cool was the military. Fighting for and defending your country was lauded, not mocked. But now patriotism is seen as a bizarre leftover novelty from a bygone era—like tiki bars and ulcers. Yet the veterans I meet seem so much more interesting than the dopes who mock them. A veteran garners strange new respect, the kind afforded to mystical beings returning from the dark side. Sadly, it used to be cool to export freedom worldwide; now it's way cooler to import its opposite to our shores.

The first step in dismantling America's greatness is dismantling the idea that America was and is great to begin with. Just referring to yourself as "an American" has become silly, an act relegated to trailer parks and country music stars.

No matter what America does in regard to foreign policy, it is "warlike." We are now governed by people who believe that simply protecting ourselves is an aggressive move against a gentler world. In the land of cool, we are Goliath, and the people who want to kill us are David. The cool must do everything possible to emasculate the evil giant, even if it means our eventual demise.

A recent example: The House Democrats have introduced legislation to create something called "the Department of Peacebuilding"—a federal-level agency designed to scale back our military, as well as deal with other vile crap, like (you guessed it) bullying. The implication is that our military is just a macro version of the football jock lurking outside homeroom, waiting to dunk your head in a men's room urinal, an act I often looked forward to.

Congresswoman Barbara Lee, who represents Oakland (a notoriously peaceful place, of course), had this to say:

> We invest hundreds of billions each year in the
> Pentagon, in war colleges, military academies, and
> our national defense universities, all to develop war
> tactics and strategies . . . Now we need that kind of
> investment in peace and nonviolence here at home.
>
> This culture of violence that we live in is un-
> acceptable . . . and it is far past time we address it as
> a nation.

Yeah, "a culture of violence." This coming from a woman who in the early days worked with the Black Panthers and later was a fan of Occupy Wall Street (something she lauded, as it left a trail of tears—and feces—throughout her city).

But let's address the name first, "The Department of Peace-building." The title brings to mind an ancient Gutfeld rule: Anything that a third-grader could come up with will inevitably kill you. "Department of Peacebuilding"? What's next? "The Organization of Soft Hugs and Butterfly Kisses"? "The Association of Group Sharing and Therapeutic Massage"? This crap is worse than weapons of mass destruction. For no matter how cool it is to be for peace, you can't keep the peace without a piece. These idiots wish to disarm us in order to appease our enemies. Unarmed, we are that much more pleasing to the people who want us dead. Barbara Lee is just making it easier for those who hate us to meet their goal, which is our annihilation. It's the first initiative she's championed that has any chance of success, actually. Incompetence, minus competition, always succeeds. Then destroys.

But we know that keeping the peace can only happen through our awesome ability to make war. It's not a cool thing to say. In fact, it's anti-cool to admit that without our military, we'd all be speaking Esperanto (which is the official language of Vermont,

I'm told). It's amazing that after beating Hitler, among other thugs, we still elect morons who don't get it. Why is that?

Because peace sells to kids, who see pacifism as a cooler alternative to evil warmongering soldiers. To the cool, the world would be a better place if America just stopped trying to defend America. Giving peace a chance, to them, means we'd all get along, rather than get run over by heathens. For younger people, bored by history and unencumbered by truth, how could this be wrong? It would be hilarious, if it weren't so damn dangerous.

It's not like we don't have evidence of the perniciousness of this stupid behavior. Whenever a Western peace group goes abroad, two things happen. They become propaganda tools for the enemy—or worse, hostages that we have to pay millions to get back.

Pacifists may be cool, but they are leeches. For them to exist you need nonpacifists willing to die. There's another Gutfeld rule: The number of pacifists increases in direct proportion to their distance from the danger (or their proximity to the faculty lounge—same thing really). It's an ideology better suited as artwork taped to a parent's refrigerator, but instead it's born from the academic media complex that firmly believes America is at fault. Anti-Americanism gives you cool cred (especially when you're a celebrity on foreign soil), as it helps you ignore the real evil simmering around the world. It's why every college student comes home for the holidays with dumb ideas about the world. Everything that has brought them to their fortunate spot in life becomes detached from the very entity that allowed their comfy lifestyle to happen—*the big fucking army that protects us.*

Remember that Barbara Lee voted against the authorization of force following the attacks on 9/11. She was the only person in both Houses to do so, making me think that she would have tried to combat Hitler with a Whitman's Sampler. She believes that surrender beats security, proving that peaceniks cause more war because they lure the bad guys into thinking we are just as dumb as the pacifists. And ultimately, pushovers. I would tell her to go to hell if she didn't already live in Oakland.

But when you eliminate patriotism because it's uncool, what do you replace it with? If we are not Americans, then what are we? Well, we are increasingly becoming things that have nothing to do with character. Patriotism is now replaced with pigment. Exceptionalism is now supplanted by orientation. We no longer take pride in a national identity but instead proclaim attributes that aren't really attributes at all—descriptors that require no achievement. It's now cool to be somebody and, like socialism, eliminate the forward pull of a meritocracy. You're great because you're black; you're great because you're a lesbian; you're great because you're Eskimo, dyslexic, androgynous, Hispanic, Celtic Wicca. But get this—ultimately there will be people better than you are at a job, and not beholden to these ideas. And in a few years, they're all going to be laughing at us in Mandarin, Hindi, or Brazilian Portuguese. Why do I doubt that the BRIC economies are starting up any Institutes of Peace Studies? The best competitive investment they could make would be to fund ours. They'll be laughing themselves silly while we contemplate our "interiority."

BLING BEFORE BALLS

How has cool ruined sports (that is, everything that isn't soccer)? Well, think about what's missing in sports these days: modesty. It's gone. Modesty, after all, isn't cool. Cool is about attention-seeking, and gratification from the masses. Modesty can't compete. Which is why it's no wonder that so many millions took to Tim Tebow like the second coming of Christ. It's a testament to the times that a mediocre athlete who innocently proclaims there's something greater than himself is seen as oddly refreshing. We live in an age when blending in and being accepted require ambivalence, tacky but expensive jewelry, garish tattoos, two illegitimate kids, and a first-name-basis relationship with the local strippers.

Accompanying the death of modesty: the death of character. It's kinda scary that if you don't act a certain way, other athletes call you a "cornball" or label you a freak. It's got to be tough, I admit, for a twenty-two-year-old rookie to know that his unusual political leanings (i.e., he's not a leftist) leave him open to ridicule. Take Redskins quarterback Robert Griffin III, who said the most uncool thing a black athlete can say: "For me, you don't ever want to be defined by the color of your skin . . . you want to be defined by your work ethic, the person that you are, your character, your personality." That comment resulted in ridicule from a dipshit ESPN analyst, Rob Parker, who wondered if Griffin "was a brother or a cornball brother." Meaning, Parker questioned his "authenticity" as a cool black dude. Apparently Parker would have preferred Aaron Hernandez, and he's not even black. But maybe to Parker his litany of violence certainly screams "non-cornball."

That cool rule—that you are a "cornball" for rejecting high-risk lifestyles—sends a horrible message to kids who aren't lucky enough to be pro athletes. Reading isn't a core skill for pro athletes, to be sure, but it is for the 99 percent of student athletes who will need to read a job application one day.

A lot of the cool mystique of professional athletes originates not from the sports world but from the entertainment world. It used to be that being a pro athlete was *enough*. No longer. Simply excelling on the field is not cool anymore. Blame bling fests like *Cribs*. The athlete has learned that the attention-seeking squeakiest wheel doesn't just get the grease, it gets the groupies and the paychecks. And ultimately divorce, alimony, and rehab.

Athletes get addicted to their cool image and, once they retire, often make desperate attempts to "keep cool." For example, if you're Dennis Rodman, a man facing a life of aging irrelevance, you go to North Korea. Back in February 2013, the former US basketball star and tongue-studded buffoon visited NK with the Harlem Globetrotters on *Vice* magazine's dime, hanging out with leader Kim Jong-un. This is what happens, I guess, when the past seems better than the future.

Mind you, this visit took place right after NK released an alarming video threatening to bomb the United States, featuring footage of our president in flames. That's kind of uncool, but when you're being feted by a dictator, why bring up such issues? That's totally uncool, dude. *Let's party.* Oh yeah, the country had just conducted an underground nuclear test weeks before too, but I'm sure that was only for fun. And Rodman probably thinks "underground test" is a strip club move done for men in sweatpants.

Rodman spoke to the media about Kim (a creepy tyrant who's become a bedsore on the earth's ass) at the Sunan Airport as he left:

> The most was that one thing, you know what, it was amazing how he was so honest. And one thing that, guess what, his grandfather, and his father were great leaders. And he's such a proud man.
>
> He's proud, his country likes him, and I like him, love him, love him, guess what, yes, yes, I love him, the guy's awesome.

Translation: Come on, guys, he's cool. He's the president (or something like a president) of a giant country! That's cool! And it's cool that I get to hang with him (unlike you). Further translation: "I can't rebound anymore, so I need to do *something* to stay famous. I'd eat a live ferret for another fifteen minutes of attention. And to be honest, I'm kind of hungry."

After the idiocy broke, Rodman faced a barrage of criticism. He appeared on ABC's *This Week* with George Stephanopoulos to try to justify his bizarre lovefest with a petulant, diminutive monster (Kim, not Stephanopoulos). He wore sunglasses and dressed in a garish jacket and baseball cap. (Cool rule number one: Play by your own rules! Screw those stiffs in suits!) When

George asked Dennis why he'd travel to a place with such a horrible record on human rights, bringing up its death camps, Rodman replied that "we do the same things here." Which qualifies him as a Huffpo columnist, right there.

Does this stuff sound familiar? The celebrity naivety? The relativism? The "we are no better than they are" line? Dennis Rodman is a Lillian Hellman who could rebound (except Rodman's prettier). He's Jane Fonda with a jump shot. He's Sean Penn with a nose ring and a catalog of sorry tattoos. He's no rebel. He's just another celebrity who, addicted to cool, is willingly duped into any kind of phony propaganda. Just make this guy feel special, and he will say anything about you (provided you pay his way and make sure he flies first-class). He will love you. He will defend you. He will think you're cool. I'd tell Rodman that he's a poor man's Walter Duranty, but he'd only say, "Inka dinka doo." Which, by the way, he often does say, when he's not saying "awesome."

Of course Rodman probably saw very little of North Korea, but he might have read a little history. He was, like so many apologists, up on his relativistic game—responding to the death camp accusation with an accusation of American guilt. When all else fails, pull that "we're just as bad" card, because it's the coolest thing to say when you have nothing else to say. I call these morons "dictatortots," for they act like children in the face of seductive, coercive power. They just don't know any better. But they know one thing: It's cool to be liked; it's cool to get attention, even if it's from someone who leaves a trail of starved bodies in his wake.

Today, Rodman is just another example of the sad kind of "thinking" that now comes from our athletes. I get it coming from professors, grad students, and bad actresses. Athletes, who spend their lives working hard and understanding the nature of achievement, should know better. But as we move farther and farther away from the real meaning of sportsmanship, this is what you get: Rodman indulging a maniac, while denigrating the country that made him rich. If Kim is so great, and "we're no better," why isn't he hanging around strip clubs in Pyongyang instead of Miami? Maybe because in North Korea, the models aren't anorexic by *choice*.

Recently I asked a pal of mine who played pro baseball, Rico Brogna, about the difference between great athletes and their lesser peers. "The best performers realize the value of being rewarded for their hard work and don't take it for granted. Players want to play, simply stated . . . they don't want to do any other outside crap, they just want to work out and play their sport." Those athletes seem to be as rare as a Tim Tebow touchdown.

Locker rooms are now full of stunted adolescents chasing fame and wealth, when—as Rico says—they should be keeping their eye on the ball. Because the game is no longer enough, athletes spend more time cultivating a shallow persona to elevate their cool profile. And this explains the tacky clothes, the awful cars, the horrendous jewelry, and all the perpetual rap sheets. In an effort to create an identity, so many athletes have adopted the *same* identity: the bejeweled, club-happy, limousine-loving lout, more enthralled by attention than achievement. You can't blame all of them. They became rich before they became men. And generally, because they never become the latter, they lose the former too.

But if you want to look for real character, and real grace in sports, I have one suggestion: the NCAA girls' bowling finals. I'm watching it now on television, and I'm entranced by these glorious teams of girls in skirts and shirts . . . bowling. Mind you, none of these girls have swimmer bodies. They don't have gymnast bodies. They don't have masculine frames that suggest months of steroid abuse. Most of them are of average build—a few are chubby, others are just big-boned. In a word, they are normal. Delightfully normal. And so uncool. Some could kick my ass (a man can fantasize). I just love how much fun they're having and how unassuming their fun truly is.

As I watch the girls (it's Vanderbilt vs. Nebraska—two states I've never visited), I'm thinking: Why do they seem so cool to me? It leads me to think: Where did they learn to bowl? A bowling alley, I know—but who taught them? I may be wrong, but I conclude that these girls have awesome relationships with their parents and especially their dads. Bowling is family activity. It's something you do on a weekend or on your birthday with your folks. And chances are it was the dad who got you into bowling—it's the thing you can do with a girl that doesn't involve dolls and their ridiculously complex dollhouses. I notice there are men in the crowd, with painted faces, cheering them on. I'd paint my face for them too. These women may never make the money that Rodman did, and squandered on booze and drugs, but something tells me they don't need to. Whatever they have already is more than enough: a sense of grace, modesty, and character you can only find in a place where you wear other people's shoes.

SOUTHERN DISCOMFORT

What is the South?

Ask any mediocre comedian, and within seconds he'll fart an incest joke. It's the stinky, default punch line for hacks until they find themselves headlining somewhere scary in Alabama. Then it's nervous jokes about city folk.

And if you ask anyone in media about the South, they might start humming the theme to *Deliverance*, following up with a line about "squealing like a pig." It's the go-to laugh-getter for lazy minds with high school intellects. (Me included.)

To them, the South is just the opposite of the cool and the hip. Unless, of course, the cool and the hip adopt the Southern routine ironically. You've seen it: shootin' pool; drinkin' cheap beer; growin' a beard; wearin' sleeveless T-shirts in Bushwick, Williamsburg, or any other hip enclave outside Manhattan; droppin' your *g*s in bestselling books by sexy talk show hosts.

When people rag on the South, they're using it as a proxy for everything else that we've come to define as uncool: family, church, tradition, fattening food, guns, outdoor dogs, sweet tea, and Walmart as a shopping destination and meeting place for families and friends.

And what is the South known for, in a good way? Manners. Is it any wonder, as the South goes, so goes the way we treat one another generally? In the South, people still call you sir or ma'am, and it's not just when highway cops ask you to slowly exit your car (I was only adjusting my zipper). But there's nothing cool about "please" or "thank you." If anything, manners are now employed only by the scarred, depraved villains in movies, as an ironic precursor to violent flourishes that pass as edgy comedy. The meaning: Anyone who happens to be polite is probably also a predator or a pervert or both.

Family values, holding hands, and saying grace at dinner—you can call that backward-ass, but *Duck Dynasty* is on to something. (Its phenomenal ratings can attest to that, as well as the public's visceral, angry reaction to Phil Robertson's temporary suspension.) The South has got some great employment stats, and primarily Republican governors attracting new businesses and new citizens. It's working. Which is maybe why the cool need to ridicule it so much.

In the South, in any restaurant, you might see a family praying before their meal. This is about as anathema to the New York hipster as watching FNC with an armed pro-lifer. All at once it's laid out: an intact family, platters of fattening foods, affordable clothing worn without the requisite sense of irony, and religion. God, how uncool is that! Why can't they all just go away and let us live our lives without them reminding us of all the things we've happily rejected in favor of ironic sideburns?

Living in the South, unless it's Austin, is the equivalent of attending Scarlet Letter U, for Uncool.

A California real estate firm called Movoto proved how acceptable it is to defecate all over a large swath of the country. They ran an article listing the most "redneck" cities in the country. They made their choices based on a very specific criterion: a list of attributes you could probably guess without reading the next sentence. But here it is: "Redneck" was defined by the number of Walmarts, the number of NASCAR tracks, and the number of people who didn't finish high school. Also included: how many taxidermists, gun stores, and country music stations. Yep, if you're a typical Southerner, right now you're cleaning your Gatling to the sound of Larry Gatlin under the frozen stare of a stuffed deer. You're probably also chewing tobacco and spitting it on the floor, next to your inbred cousin who's having sex with a chicken.

Anyway, Atlanta won the prize as most redneck, but the runners-up included Kansas City, Oklahoma City, Nashville, and Tulsa.

Before I go on, you gotta ask yourself: What kind of real estate firm would go to the trouble of denigrating markets where there is viable real estate? It's as if they were saying, "This market is too uncool for us. We only sell refurbished Victorians in the Haight." Problem is, that's not just bad business, it's bigoted business. It's like a barber banning the high and tight—not the best way to build a customer base.

I called the real estate company and asked their publicity guy why they chose to do this article. He said they thought it would be funny and might generate some buzz. Which it did. I crapped all over the firm on *The Five*.

I asked the guy if they thought "redneck" was pejorative, and he said no. Then I asked him why adjacent to the article, the

177

website featured *that* scene from *Deliverance*—the odd-looking kid with the banjo. Was that supposed to be a *positive* representation of the South?

The poor guy stuttered a bit and conceded that, no, comparing places to a crazy, violent hillbilly culture isn't exactly a valentine.

And then I asked him if they would consider doing the equivalent for blacks. Would his company ever do the country's most "hip-hop" or "gangsta" cities to live in? You see, I was trying to drum up a similar but politically more tenuous version of their white stereotype. Obviously new to the public relations game, the chap said, honestly, that they had considered doing that. But changed their minds, because it would be seen as, well, unseemly.

I gently eased the poor guy into observing his company's own hypocrisy. I have to say, even I felt bad for him. But then I thought: Screw him. It's okay to call a Walmart shopper a redneck, but you can't call a fan of sagging pants gangsta? How are these two things different?

They are because you can get away with the former and you'll lose your job at a dinky real estate website if you attempt the latter.

But it seems to me that a lot of the most uncool stuff happening around our country isn't occurring anywhere in the South. Let's pick two recent examples: the Ariel Castro sex dungeon in Cleveland and the Kermit Gosnell abortion house of horrors in Philly.

Both are not in the South. Both are in actual "cities"—places where people have full sets of teeth and pedigree dogs you carry when you're shopping.

I didn't pick those two horrible events out of thin air. I picked them because both abysmal stories unfolded in cities leisurely. These crimes occurred unabated for, like, ever.

How does that happen? Seriously, do you think you could run a rape dungeon in the South for a decade? I doubt it. People tend to visit their neighbors, hang around, and *know* the turf. I would expect in the South, as well, they'd pretty much glom on fast if an abortionist was murdering living, breathing kids. Southern hospitality means looking out for one another. Sure, they know when to mind their own business. But they also have a tight-knit community, often centered on a church. Some might call it nosy, but that nosiness can be lifesaving.

As once-vaunted cities decay and rust (the list is longer than my bar bill), and their once-bustling populations exit to safer places, we are left with urban dead zones—vast spaces where the people who live there keep to themselves. These are cities predicated on not making eye contact. Ever. We create invisibility for criminality by averting our own gazes.

An entire season's plot of the HBO show *The Wire* was devoted to how gangs could dump bodies in abandoned houses in Baltimore, simply because *no one* noticed. Right now, Detroit is considering using goats and sheep to eat the overgrown grass swamping the desolate and deserted streets, avenues once populated by families. It's not a city; it's a postapocalyptic petting zoo. It's not the South that's uncool; it's the tragic urban wastelands created by decades of liberal cronyism and corruption. Japan didn't kill Detroit. Try Kwame Kilpatrick. The left has destroyed more cities than Godzilla.

On to Cleveland: How could Ariel Castro get away with his house of horrors for so long? Or his neighbor, too, who—months later—got charged with 4 counts of aggravated murder, 173 counts of rape, and 115 counts of kidnapping? Elias Acevedo Sr., who lived doors down from Castro, is accused of abusing three women for years. *What the hell is wrong with this place?* Ingrained in the city life is this: If you see something, don't say anything. The South was built on manners. In the North, it's built on mayhem. In Chicago, Detroit, and other cities, the populations are sitting ducks for predators who prowl unabated because the neighborly concern of the South does not exist.

There is nothing sadder or more sickening than the Kermit Gosnell story. If you read it as fiction—an abortion doctor snapping the spines of weeping babies—you'd think it's the plot for a *Texas Chain Saw Massacre* sequel. But it's not Texas. It's Philadelphia. There was no one there watching, worrying, or acting on a concern for others in that story.

This, in part, explains why suddenly the South seems so damn appealing, if still uncool. The South, in my mind, is the new black.

The neighbors there may have a funny drawl, but they won't turn away when you scream for help. If that's uncool, sign me up.

THE REBELS OF ROMANCE

As the sibling of three sisters, I'm an expert on bad boyfriends. I saw every kind. Druggies. Jocks. Tennis players. Ruby Tuesday waiters. But growing up, girls are always told by their dads, brothers, and uncles to steer clear of the riffraff. The bad guys traffic in cool, mimicking the bad-boy persona glamorized in movies. Shorthand: a walking sulk. Your father, if he was smart, terrorized them with a glance.

Here's what dads know: Cool is alluring when you're young, but it's not the best choice for marriage. When a man or woman settles down, they are instinctively programmed to seek out the mate that provides for them over the long term.

Yes, I know "provides" is some sexist code word for "misogynistic lady-hating bastard," but that's only because feminists made it so. Providing for someone is a sacrifice, and it's mutually selfish. That's the pact. You're a team and you provide for each other. And then, later, provide for a family. True, it sets limits to other behaviors: You can't stay out all night doing lines of coke anymore (well, unless you've got a nanny who wipes down

GREG GUTFELD

the mirror). Overall, though, the "settling down" thing is a good thing. It creates a long-term solution for something that requires a long-term solution: the mailing of your genes into the future, safely. It's actually kind of cool. And it's also pretty hard. Sometimes I think the reason why it's denigrated so much is not that it's dorky but that it's difficult. You can never be perfect at it, so why bother with it at all? You'll argue with your wife, your kids will annoy you, and it's just easier to wake up in the morning with a hangover and a hooker than with a three-year-old bouncing on your bed demanding pancakes shaped like unicorn heads. (Some things you never grow out of.) Although I know a lot of cool dads who manage to be married and still have fun (or perhaps they're just good actors). It takes the concentration, compartmentalization, and endurance of a pro athlete.

But our culture paints a picture of the stable earner husband as sooo boring (uncool). For a woman to link up with him is emotionally more devastating than the physical consequences reaped from hooking up with a freethinking activist with substance abuse problems. Face it, the paragons of pop culture (editors, artists, directors, reflexologists) really think you'd be better off marrying a goateed gun-running meth-head than the goofy husband parodied in every sitcom or crime drama. In Dick Wolf's world of *Law & Order*, it was almost certain that the well-to-do husband was a murderous pedophile, played by Rob Lowe's less successful brother. The fact that I can't remember his name tells you I'm drunk.

Hollywood likes to think it bears no responsibility for changes in society, yet that doesn't explain why it feels so strongly about calling whatever it makes "art." Their livelihoods are predicated on people *believing* they influence your life. Especially when the same messages are delivered over and over again for years.

Which is why whenever I want to make an important point about something, I immediately refer to the movie *Grease*. In the 1978 film, Olivia Newton-John plays a Goody Two-shoes Sandy Olsen, who inevitably transforms into a leather-clad sexpot. It's understood that leather thigh-highs are cooler than saddle shoes. Leather is shorthand for sex. But it's also a declaration. It signifies that everything that came before was stupid and that risky behavior trumps sanity and safety.

But where does this transformation from prim to precarious lead? What happens when you abandon traditionally boring goody-goody behavior for recklessness and "freedom"? In my mind, ironically, it leads to dependence. By sacrificing one kind of system of provision, you are forced to embrace another. And the new one is a lot less nurturing.

That sacrifice leads directly to single women embracing big government and voting for it more and more. Apparently, rebelling against your stern upbringing seems cool, but blindly taking from the government isn't. At least Mom and Dad and a husband really do honestly love you.

The original purpose of government—any government—is safety. That's why people banded together ten thousand years ago. Today, so many of us take safety for granted that the government has gone from protection provider to love provider. But it's more than that. In changing government from Mars to Venus, we've undermined Mars. He's neutered, flaccid (especially if he went to Princeton). That's the real problem, in the most basic terms. Government is spending all its money on a plethora of programs that do not really provide love or companionship. Plus, at some point the government won't be able to provide protection anymore either. The resources won't be there. Government won't be there for you when the neighbors' meth-head son climbs in your bedroom window. Nor will it be there when the Islamist or anarchists or Putin or whoever goes medieval on America. People have grown falsely secure. Which means they slept through even more of history classes than I did.

Being a single woman, like being a single man, can be pretty awesome. The freedom to do what you want is invigorating. But for many, it's a dead end, spiritually, morally, and financially. That's because most single women do not have the luxury of being Olivia Newton-John, or Madonna, or Lady Gaga. Hell, they're not even Kathy Griffin (a good thing). No, they're just some girl who made some bad decisions, and on the precipice of forty is now staring at a cat and a worn-out woman's magazine promising her eight steps to better self-esteem. Sure, she's got the birth control and the abortions covered, but being childless and single isn't as cool as promised. A desire to be cool, or accepted as cool by those who convinced you it's superior, leaves you where we all end up: alone. You're just there a heck of a lot sooner.

We tend to forget that one type of woman is still up for ridicule: the virgin. In the pantheon of uncool, they're no better off than bearded ladies at the circus—and as rare. When you actually hear about a female virgin, it's usually making headlines as a freakish anomaly. "You wouldn't believe who's a virgin," the story screams, and then it treats the female like a frog being dissected in a lab by a group of gum-smacking students. A female virgin (especially if she's attractive) is the modern woolly mammoth: usually found frozen, intact, in the Arctic. It used to be that doing something against the grain was the mark of a cool person. If the activity was something that rebelled against the rigid structure of society, it would be. And well, yeah, I guess it is. But the media refuses to see it that way. It's no coincidence that so many men decry virgins. The shorthand for the mockery is really, "Thanks for nothing, sweetie."

You want to see a confused magazine editor? To induce the kind of cognitive dissonance that results in a *Scanners*-like head explosion? Pitch him or her a story about a hot, young, successful virgin. You'll quickly find that editor's mental hard drive approximating a Fukushima meltdown.

In the world of sex, alternative sexual practices are championed if they involve masks, restraints, and multiple partners. But having no partners at all? That's the butt of withering jokes. Take the last summer Olympics, where an Olympic hurdler (and a really cute one at that) named Lolo Jones became the center of attention because of her creepy, abnormal lifestyle. In an interview on an HBO program, she admitted she was a virgin. A freakish being who decided she was not having sex until she had got a husband, because of her religious faith. Wow, a media twofer: religious *and* a virgin. Of course HBO promoted the heck out of her anomalies. The woman was suddenly the Olympian equivalent of a live yeti who plays the ukulele.

She made a choice. But it's a choice a feminist hates to hear, which I never understand. Feminists prefer to view virgins as people who are repressed rather than a smart person avoiding the mistakes made by her peers. Shouldn't they be saluting this girl for not falling prey to the male pig? Shouldn't they be shouting, "Right on, sister!" to Lolo, since she's *not* giving it to the man? Shouldn't her strength, her independence, be championed?

The same press that idolizes people with dangerous lifestyles and destructive habits views Lolo as a goofball, despite the fact that her lifestyle is infinitely healthier than all the screwups around her. Furthermore, the press elevates those who adopt healthy lifestyles in the areas of fitness and nutrition. But, if you play it totally safe—sexually, for the sake of a sound mind and body—then you're actually *unhealthy*. Think about it: If an athlete says she eats nothing but organic vegetables and fresh fish, an interviewer would be like, "Yeah, me too! We're so cool!" But say, "I'm saving myself till marriage," and that's oddly toxic. It's the kind of logic that makes food products more expensive when they leave *out* an ingredient. It's a scam, folks.

So where's the danger in this? Well, any young girl watching how Lolo is portrayed might come away with the idea that having scruples is silly. If you're having thoughts about sex when you're in high school, and girls who abstain are viewed as freakishly uncool, then what are you going to do? Your inclination, if you don't have a strong mom and dad, is to get the whole thing over with, with anyone, including a middle-aged talk show host who can buy you Zimas. (They still make Zima, right?) Being a virgin is a scarlet V, so you must lose it so you're no longer freakishly uncool. I think this explains most premature loss of virginity. It's obviously the same for guys too.

And so the concept of a great-looking woman in her late twenties saving herself for marriage seems as incongruent as a manatee in heels, and now a whole bunch of young girls might feel that way about their virginity too, especially young black women. Not that they are at risk or anything, of course.

In a book that celebrates Free Radicals, you can and should learn something by taking a deeper look into Jones's life. Here is a woman whose incredible self-control led her on a path to ridiculous achievement. She is in the fucking Olympics (not the "fucking Olympics"). Do you know any Olympians offhand? No. They don't socialize, they train. And they're rare for a reason. They make choices that allow for success. They create an athletic life that requires hard work, without temptation of weaker types who might mock them for their diligence (sounds familiar, no?). The path to glorious achievement was uninterrupted by all the crap that our insidious, shallow culture deems as cool or edgy. She adopted the hardest path and pretty much blew through the first part of her life without the usual bullshit the rest of us get mired in. Do you think she could train up to her level if she spent her weekends wrestling a has-been actor from *Entourage* in the backseat of a leased BMW? (This is why I never medalled in curling.)

Lolo is an example of what I call a "super-fact" (i.e., a really great fact): Delayed gratification *never* leads to failure in life . . . ever. Ask yourself this: Has anything ever gone wrong in your life if you put something off? I'm talking about a drink, or a drug, a cheeseburger, a random sex act. Every time I'm about to order something from Taco Bell, I think to myself, "If I'm around tomorrow, I'll do it then." And I never do. It's how I've kept my girlish figure for the last four years. I've also avoided a lot of explosive diarrhea.

And what happens when you resist?

Does your life collapse? Or do you actually get something done? Chances are you *always* do something that makes you feel better than whatever temptation you were about to succumb to. I call this the Power of Procrastination. I sense a *Dr. Phil* segment in my future.

The forgotten art of delayed gratification became forgotten because the culture of the 1960s and 1970s transmitted the message, through TV, movies, and music, that it was cool to satisfy your every whim whenever it struck your fancy. "If it feels good, do it" were six words that defined the downward slide of a culture. To test yourself against the rigors of discipline, to gain whatever prize might be waiting for you at the end, was a waste of your time.

One would be hard-pressed to find a more nihilistic, destructive philosophy. What used to be cool (and rather smart)—working, or waiting—fell under the heading of "why bother?" Anyone who, as a kid, was walking to band or soccer practice, only to be stopped by a friend wishing to do otherwise (break into a house and steal underwear), knows what I mean. "Tune in, turn on, drop out" didn't produce a nation of enlightened beings. It produced a nation that can barely read and write.

Feminists tricked women into thinking that wanting the same things as cool and careless men do, and throwing caution (and bras) to the wind, would put you in a better place. It might give you some better memories, at first, but the place you end up is never the place you expected. It's never with *that* guy. He gets what he wants and moves on. (Yes, I'm sounding like a grand-mother, but maybe I am one. I do smell an awful lot like lavender, but that's a medical disorder.)

No one wants to hear it, but the studies find what I'm getting at: Delayed gratification works. The younger you have sex, the sooner you "peak," in just about everything. You grow old too fast, and nothing seems that great as life goes on. Lolo shows you what you can do if you forget "just say no" and embrace "just not now." It allows you to get more crap done, and that allows for more freedom—freedom most feminists can never dream of. Lolo's flown all over the world because she worked hard; most feminist bloggers don't get past Penn Station when they're taking the train back home to their parents to do their laundry. Lolo's resistance to what other people define as cool has allowed her options many feminists will never, ever have. No wonder they hate her.

THE CARNAL CARNIVAL

Sex isn't supposed to be boring. But amateurs have made it so. They've turned Chris Isaak into Chris Hayes.

In March 2013 a *Guardian* article detailed a controversy that erupted at the University of Tennessee surrounding a student-led Sex Week on the campus. According to the *Guardian*—which has become the world's college newspaper—the campus extravaganza is "aimed at promoting sexual health and awareness," which, for anyone experienced in the lexicon of "awareness," is always code for frumpy, tattooed experts brandishing edible condoms and adjustable-speed vibrating dildos. The paper notes that it "had its funding slashed after Republican lawmakers launched a campaign against the event." Boo hoo, you evil Republicans, always out to squash a screw. You're like, so 1950s and repressed!

And there you have the cool/uncool narrative blossoming, in the comfortable confines of a sympathetic media that instinctively follows the scent of repression by the hands of Republicans. They can't get enough of it. To them, it's always *Footloose*—the young kids rebelling against the rigid minister who hates fun, hates kids, hates everything. He's probably closeted and sleeps with lemurs (male ones!).

The best part of this article, however, is the accompanying picture. It features two extremely solemn students (Jacob Clark and Brianna Rader) flanking a chalkboard. Both students are looking dead serious at you, as though they're staring down the tanks of Tiananmen Square. On the chalkboard between them, the word SEX is written. The board could have been the Berlin Wall, November 1989. I look at it and I hear "Heroes" playing in my brain. They really are America's brave warriors, withstanding the onslaught of . . . nothing really. What totally wasted energy. Agoraphobics take greater risks.

Yes, they were making a stand. For sex. For awareness. On . . . a college campus. Yep, a campus, where I guess no one has ever heard of sex. Where no one has ever seen a condom. Where no one has ever had sex on the floor of a sorority, and then lost their underwear while climbing out a window. (What can I say, it was past curfew.)

These are today's modern revolutionaries. While students are dying all over the world fighting for freedom, these brave souls are fighting for seminars titled "Getting Laid," "Loud and Queer," "Bow Chicka Bow Wow," and a treatise on oral sex called "How Many Licks Does It Take?" (Tip: Not many.)

Now, I'd get the coolness of this heroic stance, if it were, say, happening in Iran. You risk castration. Or you might lose a hand, which kills all chances of getting to second base and eliminates most men's most amenable partner. But in the United States, taking a stand for sexual awareness is like taking a stand for more fleas at the dog pound. They're advocating for something we've already got. I mean, really: You think our culture is undersexualized? Did you watch last year's MTV Video Music Awards? This cause is about as genuine as an Obama apology.

The eighteen grand of funding for the week was supposed to come from the school but was withdrawn after an evil Republican state senator (of course) named Stacey Campfield raised a puritanical, uncool stink. I happen to think it was pretty cool that Campfield said something (for different reasons), but I'll get to that later.

Faced with the prospect of no Sex Week, some outraged students ran to Facebook and Twitter, spreading the panic that the event was in peril. This was their Arab Spring, if by Arab you mean "hand" and by Spring, you mean "job."

The activists got the hashtag #Iwantsexweek trending on Twitter, which led to worldwide attention, including from the *Guardian*, and also from my own network (the predictable evil Dean Wormer, from *Animal House*, in this equation). This emboldened the activists, who announced their success on their website, and also encouraged idiots, sorry—people—to continue forking out dough to fund next year's Sex Week. I might offer, humbly, that perhaps this money could have gone to something more worthwhile (victims of Hurricane Sandy, the Salvation Army, my own private "Buy Greg a Robot Geisha" fund), but why rain on their self-congratulatory parade? Someone, somewhere might get an edible condom. I prefer pineapple.

The event didn't get all the money it needed. Faced with a revolt, the school capitulated and allowed up to seven grand of the student fees to pay for the fun. So, in effect, in this thoughtful sex-fest, it's the students' parents who are getting screwed first, and before it even starts. They should at least get some pictures from it. Or why not participate? Bring a blanket, Dad! Bring the dog! Bow chicka bow wow, indeed.

In the world of cool, the antisex Republican is uncool, and the pro-sex students are renegades. But here is why this is bull. Sex, as a topic for seminars on awareness or entertainment, is welcomed on campus with open arms. Sex Week is meant to "blow your mind," but this whole escapade is as shocking as Christmas.

Please, kids. Although I find the idea of seeing these organizers copulating nauseating (and I have a pretty high threshold). Rubbing a balloon on my head is more electrifying. And erotic. These students want to really shock America? Say something nice about America.

This brave stand for boning is really a way to make the organizers look cool. You are, in effect, creating a facade of cool rebellion where there is none available. This is college. What can you possibly rebel against, except leftist professors with halitosis? Now, that would be fighting the man. Because you'd be battling a real army.

When it comes to sex—and this comes from decades of horrible experience—the people who always flaunt their sexual activities are always the worst at it. Trust me, I wish I didn't know this, but I do. Meanwhile the silent types—the people who never *ever* talk about sex—those are the types who take the behavior most seriously. They are, without question, the true professionals. (I use this theory not just with sex, but with cooking, writing, stand-up comedy, guitar playing, Trivial Pursuit, singing, household repairs, murder.) The best metaphor for this is *American Idol*. Everyone who shows up there thinks they can sing. Almost all of them can't. Yet you know they told everyone they could. And then it's the quiet kid, or the homely lady, who gets onstage and knocks the song out of the park. And that song never includes "bow chicka bow wow."

And more important, anyone who actually believes that having sex is an achievement must be easily impressed by rabbits, cats, dogs, and the squirrels rutting around campus. Which is why they're almost—without question—lousy at it.

But I guess given the curriculum students are choosing from these days, sex education might be the least harmful. At least when you're learning about blow jobs, you aren't reading Karl Marx (much the same, really). The more time spent discussing anal, the less time there is for lionizing Noam Chomsky. Still, wouldn't it be slightly better if the school sponsored seminars that focused on stuff that helped you get a job not prefaced by the word "blow"? You have to have an awfully healthy trust fund for this sort of behavior not to backfire on you later.

Wouldn't it be great if the seminars were called "How to Pay Off Your Student Debt" or "Make Sure You Don't Move Back Home" or "An Apartment, a Car, a Life—In One Year." Shit, how about "How to Join a Bar Band So You Can Pay for Beer"? That is far more practical. And better for your sex life. I wish I had done that. Of course, I have no musical talent. But that didn't stop Adam Levine.

But maybe "work" *is* the goal of Sex Week. If you look at the unemployment numbers in early 2013, it's pretty scary—hovering around 25 percent for boys and girls in their early twenties. So perhaps these classes are honest-to-God job preparation. The way it looks these days, the only option most of these kids have will be on their backs. Hooking might be the new IT. It's like that scene in *The Graduate*. Forget "plastics." Maybe the old guy at the party is telling the new graduates, "sodomy." Yep, when the evil Republican state senator said, "We should be teaching these children what is important to learn so they can get jobs," he was wrong. Sorry, Senator, the way things are headed, maybe the school sees the future—and it's lubricated.

I do realize that by devoting time to Sex Week, I become, once again, the symbol of uncool: a white middle-aged guy railing against filthy kids. But I argue it's the opposite. Every professor behind this is probably my age, and totally for it. If anything, rebellion against this silliness *is* cool. Case in point, the week was supposed to feature a poetry-reading lesbian bondage expert (which is a longer way of saying "bullshit artist"). And it's akin to having ants at a picnic. Totally expected. It's about as rebellious as breaking wind in a bathtub—another thing I have experience in but keep to myself. (Well, mostly. It's amazing what goes viral on German YouTube.)

Sex Week is really part of a bigger idea, a larger damaging, stupid trend that seeks to obliterate perhaps the greatest thing about sex: mystery. Mystery is the best part about sexual attraction, and it's responsible for the greatest joy in life: chemistry. Chemistry between people is more about the unspoken than the spoken. The more you talk about it (whatever "it" is), the less interesting you become. (My friends remind me of this all the time.) If you don't know this, it's because you haven't shut up long enough to appreciate silence and all it brings. And guess what: Not acting on chemistry is pretty awesome. For one, you avoid pregnancy, divorce, STDs, and lawyers who garnish your wages.

Me, I am a huge fan of sexual repression, although my definition might be different. To me, not talking about sex is just doing a favor to the people who would have to listen to you. Plus, you can never do the act justice. For me, a person who talks incessantly about their sexual exploits is no different from a guy who brags about his partying. In his head, he surely is having the time of his life. But everyone else around him wants to punch him in the face. Including his partners. It's all generally BS anyway. A waste of oxygen and energy. Sex Week personified.

We need to abandon the idea that expressing your sexuality is brave, in-your-face, or even interesting. And so my last example hails from Pittsburgh, where during an annual art school parade at Carnegie Mellon (it's always colleges), a female student dressed up as the pope, minus pants . . . or anything, for that matter, down below. She had shaved her pubic hair in the shape of a cross, and passed out condoms. The Catholic diocese asked for the college to do something, in perhaps the nicest way possible. Bishop David Zubik put it politely: "I think we all know that when we're growing up we do stupid things, but to cross over the line in this instance shouldn't happen with anybody." The college said it would review the incident, but some students didn't seem to mind, of course. "It's all in good fun and it's not meant to harm anyone," Ivy Kristov told the local station, KDKA.

Of course it is, you moron. Nothing is brave if no one seems to mind. But you know who would mind? Try pulling that in a mosque and see how far your edgy, in-your-face expressionism takes you. Shave your pubic hair into a red crescent and advocate against the hijab someplace in Lahore. Good luck with that. We'll send flowers.

Of course, no protester would have the balls to do that. Cowards only act brave when there are no consequences. Ridicule the pope? No problem. Try Mohammed? I think you'll sit that one out. It's amazing how the fear of death can bring out the prude in you.

GUNNING FOR ATTENTION

Hollywood knows that without gun violence, there would be no Hollywood. Guns are the fresh herbs sprinkled onto every film salad to give it that extra zest. Yet, how can they embrace something so romantically on-screen, only to reject it so dramatically in real life? Hollywood's schizophrenia over guns is matched only by their attitude toward taxes. Ever wonder why they film in Vancouver so often? It ain't for the beaches, I can tell you.

Celebrities demonize guns because it instantly makes them appear compassionate. But if they did the research, they'd find that where there are more guns, there is less gun crime. I've done the math. It's not hard. I'll direct you to the research, simply google this name: John Lott Jr.

And ask any criminal (which some actual researchers have done) and they'll tell you: Knowing a victim might have a gun dissuades them from approaching that victim. But research on gun control is nowhere near as cool as screaming "guns kill children" and demanding action on Twitter, in between therapy sessions and Pilates. Witness the latest celebrities participating in gun control PSAs. Most at one point in their career rely on armed security to handle all their safety needs. If only we were all like Beyoncé, then we could marry a very rich man (and ex-criminal) who has an arsenal. Jay-Z has ninety-nine problems, but not owning a gun isn't one. Bottom line: The argument ends with "Guns are bad. Guns kill people. End of story." This passes as intellectual thought for Sarah Silverman. By the way, if feminism means women are now free to be as stoned as men have traditionally been, congrats, Sarah. You're the Rosa Parks of pot.

But we know that these asshats are living a lie. I can't think of a single television network that is housed in a building that's considered a "gun-free zone." This is where the cool are really dangerous: They embrace symbolic, worthless goals like gun-free zones and banning ornamental rifle add-ons as a measure of achievement, unaware that their fact-free opinions may in fact be part of our safety problem. Those opinions are making everyone less safe.

A "gun-free zone" is the safest place for a maniac to kill people. But cool people don't get it. They never do. In the world of common sense, they are woefully unarmed. But it's not like they hang out in high schools or malls anyway (unless they're looking for their next date). As for this preoccupation with rifles dressed up like "assault rifles," those are not the weapons killing thousands of black kids every year in every major city. But let's not touch that—it just embarrasses the liberal mayors of every city where illegal handguns turned their streets into war zones far more dangerous than the roads of Iraq. But still not as bloody as a Quentin Tarantino flick.

Meanwhile, as former New York City mayor Michael Bloomberg went to war on gun owners, Governor Andrew Cuomo made an exemption for Hollywood—allowing them to use fake weapons in the city. (These are real weapons minus ammo.) So let me get this straight—we ban guns, but encourage movies glorifying guns? Only on the coasts does this make sense. Is there an idiot molecule in seawater?

No issue creates more dishonest, self-promoting bullshit than gun control. I don't even know why it's called gun control. We don't call automotive safety "automotive control," do we? We are totally fine with speed limits (except for Sammy Hagar), and we buckle up. Safety assumes you have the right to make your decisions. Gun control implies gun owners don't have the brains to handle the same responsibility (when oddly, lawful gun owners treat guns more respectfully than Hollywood actors treat their wives). This is just more received wisdom from the regulatory state. Miramax and Harvey Weinstein deciding public policy—I'm sure that's what our founding fathers had in mind. A junta of jackasses.

Yet, when a tragic massacre like Sandy Hook hits the news, distraught and intellectually shallow emotions erupt from the usual groups—emanations that are heartily encouraged by babbling news coverage—resulting in a spasm of self-righteous sanctimony and mindless condemnation. It's a response as guaranteed as a nonsense tweet from a celebrity.

Following horrible events like Sandy Hook, there are sincere responses, of course. And then there are certain celebrity responses, designed to elevate the profile of the responder.

From Hollywood, we get opportunists who choose to make noise after such violence, because it makes them appear smart and caring, which elevates their cool factor among their equally clueless peers. To these people, a tragedy is really just a fashion accessory—one that you don't have to return Monday morning with Russell Brand's DNA all over it.

They'll make a video, even, to show how much they care, and

how great they look while they show you they care. It's also just a great time to meet up with like-minded lightweights, look each other in the eye, and validate one another's sensitive and superior persona. It's their version of a picnic.

And if you're Jim Carrey, you'll take to Twitter to insult your average gun owner—even vowing to make a song about them.

A tweet from him, to the world, the morning of March 24, 2013, read as follows:

> 'Cold Dead Hand' is abt u heartless motherf%ckers unwilling 2 bend 4 the safety of our kids. Sorry if you're offended by the word safety! ;^}

You can credit Twitter for a lot of things, but one thing they nailed for sure: As a celebrity-moron revealer (CMR), it is second to none. Twitter is celebutard Luminal. It reminds us that no matter how rich and famous a celebrity becomes, their success never makes them smarter. As the bank account skyrockets, their IQ sinks like a doomed soufflé. And the beauty of it is that it's the celeb who's actually volunteering the proof of their idiocy. (The emoticon's a good tip too.)

Carrey had promised to release an anti-gun song in a few days, and that he did, a painfully unfunny screed with a vaguely catchy melody and a safe, mocking tone dripping with adolescent irony. The song focused on ridiculing the memory of the late great Charlton Heston, as well as mocking American gun owners, millions of faceless people he paints as rednecks. Weird how so much gun crime has destroyed cities like Chicago and Detroit, but Carrey would never make a video about that. Gang crime? That's just too dangerous for Jim to lampoon. Primarily because it's not a white phenomenon. It's much easier for this Canadian with dual citizenship to smear the target that cool kids love to hate: the South and the Midwest. It's easy when you don't know any people there, and the only real citizenship you have sets its perimeters within Malibu, Miami, and Manhattan. But, unlike a good Smith & Wesson, this idiocy always backfires.

If you saw the video, Carrey apes his way through it as a cadaverous Heston impersonator, like a reject from a seventh-grade talent show. "Cold Dead Hand" has Carrey joyfully postulating that Heston liked guns because he had a tiny dick, and that he's probably rotting in hell for his work for the NRA. Carrey also mocks and parodies the show *Hee Haw*, failing to realize that *Hee Haw* already was a parody of the South. Like everything Jim does, it comes off as old and he comes off like a douche the size of a dirigible. I mean, really, the guy's been pulling the same face for twenty years now. Did we really need a modern Charlie Callas? One every two hundred years or so seems fine, doesn't it?

Now, I was never much of a gun lover. The last gun I owned was a rifle, back in 1986. Gun rights were never a core issue for me, but Carrey and self-righteous, empty-headed gasbags like him have put me there. Just looking at Carrey makes me want to buy an arsenal. I see how much they despise people like you and me, and I think, "Damn, I need to protect myself from those mindless jackasses."

This is Hollywood with its slip showing. Jimmy's video is really just his diary, open to the chapter titled "What I Really Think of Flyover America: It Reeks."

Oh yeah, these LA pricks will take your cash any chance they get—they love your money. But God, do they hate you. They're not just anti-South, they hate the Midwest, the Mid-north, the Northwest—any place where a drawl might peek out from a cheek.

But the worst part for me—the thing that got me sputtering like a parrot with Tourette's when I discussed it on TV—was the careless, vicious mockery of a dead and decent man. I get it—Carrey is a clown, and clowns clown, but at least hit someone who can hit back. Heston is dead, you pathetic coward.

Which leads me to reiterate to my friends in Hollywood—where the hell are you? If you worked with Heston, or admired him or respected what he did for civil rights in the sixties (the guy marched with Martin Luther King, unlike all of the posers in Hollywood), you should speak up and call out Carrey for the shitbag he is. Hollywood should treat him the way Lillian Gish treated Robert Mitchum in *The Night of the Hunter*: Shoot him in the ass with ridicule until he scampers into the woods screaming.

Speaking of shooting, I'll listen to nearly all opinions on guns, and even see value in ones I am diametrically opposed to. Bob Beckel thinks *all* guns could be banned, and I think it's crazy, but I know he's sincere and would like nothing better. (Well, I can think of a few things he would like better, but I'm not going there.) At least he doesn't pretend to be for something just to get attention or win votes. Whatever your opinions on guns are, it's Carrey's methods that are the issue. They reveal how shut off Hollywood is from you and me. Carrey thought his crap would be greeted with accolades, but it was met with a vibrant flush of the national toilet. And he was the turd. He should use all the yoga he practices to pull his head out of his rectum.

And given Carrey's career's downward trajectory, I wonder if his activism will just "naturally" go away. A few months after his attack on Heston and gun owners, he issued a seemingly sincere apology on Twitter. Did the apology come from his heart? Or his wallet? Was he apologizing simply because no one is going to

his movies and his attacks on law-abiding citizens didn't help? He
tweeted:

> Asslt rifle fans, I do not agree wth u, nor do i fear
> u but i do love u and I'm sorry tht in my outrage I
> called you names. That was wrong.

It's amazing what a nervous agent can get you to do.

HOMAGES TO HOMICIDES

Sorry, I'm not done with guns.

So, why is it that when a gun massacre occurs, it's the NRA that's vilified? But when gun murders reach scary proportions in places like Chicago, DC, or Detroit, no one says a thing?

Let's dissect it. Chicago crime is "just gangs." And gangs are minorities, using illegal weapons. That's a hairier situation for the cool to address. One, the shooters are nonwhites, and no one wants to appear racist condemning them. Add to that that the guns used are illegal. Cities with the toughest gun control are, like Chicago, awash in gun crime. "If you outlaw guns, then only outlaws will have guns" might be the only bumper sticker that is 100 percent true (besides "I Brake for Renaissance Fairs"). Last, the majority of this crime occurs in towns run by liberals. You can't condemn Rahm Emanuel's horrible handiwork in Chicago if his brother, Ari, is your TV agent. You need to get the cameo in *Two and a Half Men*, so mock Texans instead.

Which is why the cool choose to vilify the redneck, and not the insane or the criminal, despite reams of evidence revealing

GREG GUTFELD

that most killers involved in the massacres of innocents are resentful oddballs or mentally ill. Instead of trying to do something about getting guns away from them, the well-protected liberal elite would rather denigrate Americans who believe in the Second Amendment. Safety for me, but not for thee. (I took Latin in high school.)

The stance that guns are responsible for only horrible events requires that the cool ignore stories that upset their assumptions. They cannot explain incidents where guns make you safer, so they choose to avoid them completely. Like the abundance of polar bears or Al Gore's madness, it's a reality the left can't see.

My favorite story took place in Springtown, Texas. On a Tuesday night around midnight, a 911 operator got a call from a distressed male. But the guy wasn't a victim, he was the suspect, a burglar reporting that he was being held captive at gunpoint by the owner of the home he had just invaded. When the home owner, James Gerow, and his son confronted the career thug (with the requisite three names), Christopher Lance Moore, and asked him why he was lurking in their house, he said, "Just unlucky, I guess." A loaded gun tends to elicit the truth.

He was outgunned because the house he picked was not one of those vaunted "gun-free zones." Yep, Christopher Moore was unlucky because the family he picked was protected. It was a good thing for the family, as even Lance admits he went to the house with "bad intentions." He certainly wasn't there to wax the floors. Very few burglars actually perform household chores. Studies prove it.

Gerow and his son cornered the thief in his own truck, and the dad told his kid to shoot Moore in the legs if he tried to escape. Which in Texas is what people call compassion. I probably would have aimed for the balls (and hit a window, or a widow).

Now, in the cool world the Gerows are uncool. They are white people with guns, which, to libs, is about as cool as debt limits or church on Sunday. If only they'd listened to celebrities spreading the gospel of gun control (who have no idea what the average citizen must deal with), who knows how things would have turned out. Bad intentions might have become a bad reality. But luckily, the words of Piers Morgan hold no sway in Springtown.

And celebrity gun-foolery doesn't hold any sway with criminals either. The fact is, most thugs see things the Gerow way— that what's unlucky for a criminal is way lucky for the rest of us. A US Department of Justice survey of two thousand felons found that 40 percent of the convicted slimeballs said they had been deterred from committing a felonious act out of fear that their intended victim might be armed. Those are statistics every human being would understand, and want in their favor. Unless, of course, you're Piers Morgan, whose head was recently designated a "brain-free" zone.

Mark Steyn made a brilliant point regarding home invasions in England, which are dramatically higher than in the United States. Just over 10 percent of US burglaries are home invasions, but in England and Wales, it's over 50 percent. Why is that?

Well, if there is a possibility that one of those homes you're about to invade is armed, you won't invade. As we know, felons are as risk-averse as the rest of us. Steyn points out that for thieves in England, it's probably just safer to knock on the door and demand entrance than to climb through a window and set off an alarm, or cut themselves on broken glass. The great British sitcom *Peep*

Show illustrated this perfectly: A group of young thugs show up at the house of the main characters, knocking on the door, demanding their appliances. They harbor no illusions that their marks are armed.

Contrast that sensibility with the Gerow story. Gerow not only shows how guns work to save lives, but he also decimates the stereotype the cool love to propagate: that gun owners are crazy, violent yokels who collect guns the way pop stars collect STDs and DUIs.

Gerow revealed the opposite. He handled the situation in a sensible and, dare I say, merciful manner (not just for Texas). He allowed the gun to defuse the situation, keeping the thug from becoming a danger to his family and to others. One thing that gun control freaks fail to consider is that law-abiding gun owners actually abide by the law, and that includes taking basic firearms courses that teach you how it's done. I bet any actor who played an action hero would have blown off their own feet. And blamed the cops. Can you picture Matt Damon handling a real gun? Neither can he.

For me, the most recent gun bill debated in Congress came down to a simple question: Would it have prevented Sandy Hook? I don't think so. But even that's not the point, now that I think about it. The fact is we missed an opportunity for a real compromise because of hardcore ideologues like President Obama. For them, a "national conversation" is about two sides conversing: the left and the far left. An atmosphere was created where compromise became impossible. Reconciliation disappeared, and capital was squandered through mockery and spitting outrage. Say what you want about Obama—and for now, we still can—the man doesn't deal well with defeat. Bobby Knight was a better loser. And he had a better record.

Think about what you could have come up with. Perhaps a law that would enforce existing gun laws, cracking down on illegal possession of handguns by repeat offenders. Those are the thugs who murdered Hadiya Pendleton, the fifteen-year-old high school girl in Chicago who had just attended Obama's second inauguration. A gangbanger with priors shot her, with an illegal handgun. If he had been behind bars, Hadiya would be alive. Where were the gun control zealots on that one? Nursing their inauguration party hangovers.

And maybe we could have been able to create some kind of law that contained a mechanism that flags a mentally ill person when they go to purchase a gun. Who could be against that? But that's gone, friends. Gone. Yeah, we never had that "national conversation." Instead we got a pissy president, along with his adoring supporters, chiding a law-abiding population. And when the bill died, who did they blame? Americans. Why? Because the average citizen didn't trust the president's intentions. They thought he wanted to steal their guns. Can you blame them? After that unbelievably phony photo of him skeet shooting. And more important, after what he promised with Obamacare? If anything, Obamacare taught you that any promise from Obama is about as sturdy as a folding chair under Michael Moore. Damn, the Congress exempted itself from Obamacare. Never trust a chef whose employees won't eat at his restaurant.

Hence the collective shrug by the American people over the gun bill, which befuddled the cool, the media, and assorted elitist gun-haters on both coasts. And it ain't easy to get 314 million people to shrug all at once. It hasn't happened since the final *Sopranos* episode. Fact is, the gun control zealots just don't know any of these people who "cling" to their guns, despite there being something like 300 million firearms in this country legally. They never really took the time to see what might work. Instead, they chose symbolism over substance. They wrote the law fast, to take advantage of catastrophe, rather than writing a law to save lives. And they ridiculed people who were listening. What kills me is that it would have been really awesome to have found a way to keep guns out of the hands of crazy people: the weirdos who pulled off Sandy Hook, the Aurora killings, the Gabby Giffords shooting, the Navy Yard massacre. These horrible events are rare, and, as Nick Gillespie points out in *Reason*, not increasing over time either. But they do share a common piece: The perpetrators are nuts. I get it that it's hard to find a crazy needle in a haystack of millions, but that's way more realistic than banning all guns. *That* ain't gonna happen, people. It's like the United States winning the World Cup. Every now and then the topic gets raised by the true believers, only to have the pipe dream crash on the hard rocks of reality. And Brazilians who can kick a ball six hundred yards with their big toe.

Instead, by clinging to the idea of banning assault rifles, we missed a real opportunity to deal with issues in mental health. We should be safely locking up our guns, but we should also be locking up our crazy people. In New York, it's not guns pushing people in front of subways. It's psychopaths. But here, they don't get incarcerated, they run for city council.

And what about sentencing laws? Fact is, you can use a gun illegally, and use it again. And again after that. Why is there so much gang crime? Because the prisons are just temporary hostels for the hostile. Gang members don't mind getting arrested when they know prison is just a few months to get back in shape and learn a few new tricks. Prison is now a place to make criminals better at beating the crap out of you. If someone wrote a tome called *The Prison Workout*, they'd make millions. (That will be my next book!)

But instead, we focused on rifles, because that's the cool target. Not handguns, which, in the hands of criminals, play a role in most gun-related crime. Gun-related deaths involving rifles? Tiny. But let's face it, it's easier to go after the NRA than the Crips.

By the way, if I had my druthers (I actually had mine once, but they escaped), I'd invent one new gun law, and then offer a proposal to the media.

The law: Ban the phrase "gun-free zones." It is shorthand for "killing in large numbers is welcome." Whoever thought of this horrible idea really hates kids. There's nothing I like better than walking into a store that has the sign saying THE OWNER IS ARMED. I don't care if it's uncool, I feel safe when I'm there, and you should too, unless you plan to rob them or sing some Cat Stevens. Because a thug is more likely to skip that place for somewhere else that has no risk to entry. Or a weapon that might separate him from his head. Think about this: Fort Hood was a gun-free zone. Yep, in a military barracks, the guys and gals did not have their weapons with them. You think that didn't cross the mind of Major Nidal Hasan?

Incredibly, the federal government outlawed our military from carrying guns on stateside military bases. Yep, we demilitarized the military. As a result, it took civilian police officers to finally shoot Hasan and stop the killing—because none of his military targets could defend themselves. I'm only surprised our government hasn't banned our combat troops overseas from carrying guns. It's such a hostile gesture when you get right down to it.

Also, as part of my proposal, I politely ask the media to stop obsessing over massacres. It's time to report it, then leave it. The blanket coverage only encourages more crime. It's been reported that the Sandy Hook fiend was invigorated by the Norway shooter. He kept clippings of previous massacres. I can't help but think that this is how life's losers work, suicide by media. Explosive, memorable crime amplified by the media is the surest way to reach immortality and fame. (It certainly isn't talk show hosting, I'll tell you that.) And it's an act encouraged by the media's hopeless desire for psychoanalysis and search for root causes. And Hollywood doesn't help by making movies seeking to understand the killers (rather than their victims). Mark my words, there will be a movie about the Boston bombing, and the younger brother will be portrayed as sympathetically as Old Yeller.

Forget all the root causes: the video games, violent movies, and bullying. For creeps, massacres are a method of achieving immortality. They knew that after their colorful demise, some independent filmmaker might make a movie about them. Which is why I now bring up Gus Van Sant—the coolest of the cool in film—who made the 2003 film *Elephant*, which chronicles a fictional event based on the Columbine school massacre.

The film makes the killers the stars and creates plot points that might be considered "controversial." He makes one of the two killers, Alex, a frustrated artist suffering from being misunderstood and maligned. The implication: It's really our fault. If only we'd understand the sensitive lads among us better, there wouldn't be dead bodies all over the place.

Van Sant's perspective masquerades as controversial, when it's really just horribly mundane. But in the arts community it's cool, even winning the Cannes Film Festival's Palme d'Or in 2003. (Which is French for "gold-plated horseshit.")

Did this movie do anything to help understand why these massacres occur? I doubt it. If anything, by making a movie seeking to understand the mind-set of a fiend, it only energizes those contemplating similar actions in real life. You know, real life. That place where the Gus Van Sants of the world don't seem to live.

This did not happen on-screen. On March 21, 2005, Jeff Weise, sixteen, killed his grandfather and the grandfather's companion, then went to a high school and killed five students, a teacher, and a guard, before he turned the gun on himself. According to CBS News, "It was the worst US school shooting since the attacks by a pair of students at Columbine High in Colorado in 1999."

And according to WCCO-TV, friends had met with Weise at a pal's house seventeen days prior to the massacre, to watch "the award-winning" movie *Elephant*. I guess that's called preparation. I mean, if it were *Sixteen Candles* or *Red Dawn*, I'd let it slide.

Weise was simply looking at the fruits of his future endeavors. Watching Van Sant's flick, he might have thought that one day a movie would be made about him, and that movie would seek to understand *him*. And that's what this is really about: massacre as performance art by monsters, reinterpreted by artists as tragic circumstances born from a brutal, bullying society. Screw the French—*that* should win an Oscar! Finally, I am cool—even if I'm dead.

One question worth asking: Why didn't Van Sant simply follow the script in front of him? Meaning, why didn't he just do the facts? Was a story about two fiends meticulously planning a horrible crime just too simplistic? Was there not enough gray area to make it an intellectual exercise? Was the concept of evil inflicting horror on the innocent not edgy enough to win an award? How would Gus have handled a story on the Mansons? Just a misunderstood family trying to make it work in the desert? Someone tell Ashton Kutcher to start growing the beard.

THE ORIENTATION EXPRESS

Train has pulled out of the station.

The station being the 2013 National Scout Jamboree, which is the yearly Boy Scout meet that draws over fifty thousand participants and their adorable decorative badges. (I have a dozen—badges, not Boy Scouts.) This year the band Train (of which I am a fan) decided that, based on the Scouts' position on gays, it would be best to cancel their appearance at the event. Originally booked for the concert in West Virginia, Train, along with something called Carly Rae Jepsen (if I knew who she was, I would be a thirteen-year-old girl, which has been my dream since I was twelve), decided to withdraw to avoid being viewed as agreeable to the Scouts' intolerant views. They couldn't afford to be on the wrong side of this issue. And I don't blame them. Remaining on the bill could revoke their cool card forever. They'd be stuck playing local fairs, like my uncle Steve. He's written an entire opera for the spoons. It's six hours long.

So, cool. That's their choice. And I like Train, and consider

Pat Monahan a pal. He's been a friend to my show, and put up with my nonsense on more than one occasion. He even wrote a pretty good song about *Red Eye*. ("It's what you watch when there's nothing else on." I'll take it.)

The only problem with his decision is that his band still played at the Dubai International Jazz Festival in Dubai Media City, in the United Arab Emirates, the next week. The cheapest price I could find was £105, but "platinum standing" will cost you £255, which by my calculations is about seven million dollars. I'd love to go, but I have a problem with Dubai (for one, too many vowels). I believe alcohol is banned there (although I hear that that ban is no longer observed). To me, that's hell. I'd rather spend a weekend in a metal box listening to Carly Rae Jepsen.

The point is Dubai is way more intolerant than the Boy Scouts. Their policy on homosexuality is a bit more strict than what's prohibited around Eagle Scouts. The UAE says that sexual relations outside of heterosexual marriage are against the law, a crime punishable by deportation, jail, listening to Carly Rae Jepsen, and even death. Unlike the Boy Scouts, if you're gay and caught in the UAE, you may be forced to undergo hormone treatments, which could include chemical castration, which, in my view, seems a tad extreme (and I like chemicals). The laws don't stop there. You can also be charged with adultery if you're married and are caught having same-sex relations. All in all, it's not really the Middle East, it's the Middle Ages. It's been reported that while such behavior is outlawed, it's pretty much ignored (perhaps for financial reasons), but still, there it is. In black and white. If you're gay, they hate you. How is this different from South Africa during the apartheid era?

So, why the heroic stance against the Boy Scouts, but not the gay-haters in Dubai? The answer is simple: No one cares about Dubai. Most think it's a cologne. So a band can get away with the hypocrisy and still make the big bucks.

Crapping on the Boy Scouts is just way easier, and cooler. It's the in thing to do these days, along with dog tattoos, drinking coconut water, and drinking coconut water with your tattooed dog. The Boy Scouts must be evil. They're just so . . . Caucasian.

For the boycotter, what happens in America is always worse than what happens anywhere else. And if you're a pop star, you have to play the game. The pressure to conform to the rising tide of indignation against the Boy Scouts requires an artist to act the part. But anywhere else where "cultures are different"? They can get around it. The Emirates' prejudice is just a cultural quirk. (Castration of gays? A bit of delightful color. Unless, of course, it's you that Achmed is coming for with a rusty scalpel.)

But seriously, Train: If you're going to drop the Scouts, you have to drop the burka crowd too. It only makes sense, right? At least the Boy Scouts do great stuff for boys, here in America. They don't spend their lives buying seven-figure cars and filling them with trucked-in models who mistakenly thought they won a beauty pageant.

Train isn't the only band that plays it both ways. But in the modern and healthy era of gay rights, all is forgiven if you go after the easy targets, like the Boy Scouts. And Boy Scouts should never be easy targets, except for Girl Scouts.

Which leads me to gays in general. And in particular, gay marriage. Lots of straights loudly embrace this issue because it functions as a "stamp of cool." If you're for gay marriage, then you're forgiven for everything else. It's the code word you need to enter the tree house of tolerance. Most of these straights would never be so forthcoming on other issues. But on this one they will become politically outspoken, because it's cool and you're in no position to lose anything. You could be a human trafficker who uses nuns for target practice, but be a vocal gay marriage supporter and you will never brunch alone.

It's the right position, in my opinion. And I'm not saying it to be cool. After you read the following paragraphs, you'll agree. My support for gay marriage is about as uncool as it can get.

I'm for gay marriage because I'm a pig. And a conservative. As a conservative, I support marriage over promiscuity. If you accept homosexuality as a biological fact, then the next step is wondering how, in this new world, one can lead a healthy life if you're a dude who likes sleeping with other dudes. My theory is: A dude is a dude, gay or straight—and as dudes, we are pigs. Left to our devices, we'd stick our penises in pottery if it had the right curves. (I can confirm this.) We'd rut with a woolly mammoth if we were drunk on triple mai tais and found one of these hairy hunks defrosting in the Antarctic. When I was a kid I was hopelessly attracted to the bendy legs of living room sofas. It's why I was no longer allowed in Pier 1 Imports. (Isn't it time they lifted that ban? There have been no issues for at least six months.)

What marriage does for straight men—narrowing choice and creating a structure that encourages and preserves a healthy, prosperous life—should be available to men who prefer other men. And if two ladies want to get hitched, go for it. Maybe because I'm more worried about straight marriage than gay marriage. As divorce rates rise, and illegitimacy rates skyrocket, it's pretty clear the disintegration of marriage is not a promising path for all involved. Why ban something for others that keeps the rest of us from destroying ourselves?

And I'm also for gay marriage because I'm a libertarian. Who the hell am I to tell you who to wed? It's hard enough to figure

out how men and women can live together without expressing opinions on two very happy men trying to make a go of it.
There are no experts in the mess of human relations. Look at
Dr. Phil. He's an expert. If that's a paragon of advice, then we're
all screwed. I wouldn't ask him how to floss.

But just because you're cool for being pro–gay marriage, does
it make everyone who disagrees with you uncool? I don't know. I'd
say a lot of them are uncool, but a lot of them are cooler than you.

This is all pretty new, when you think about it. Earthlings
have been around for some two hundred thousand years (I don't
have exact numbers due to the vodka) and gay rights didn't hit
the planet until maybe the last forty years. Can you blame everyone for not immediately coming to grips with the biggest shift in
biological reconsideration to happen since we lost our tails? Can
you blame people who are being asked to suddenly disavow the
beliefs that have governed not just their own actions, but their
ancestors', for taking a while to consider their position? It's easy
and cool to call them bigots and close-minded a-holes, but it wins
no friends. And it's wrong. Most of them are decent people contemplating a seismic shift in world belief. Just because you didn't
ascribe to that belief doesn't mean you can dismiss their concerns
so easily.

In my rattled head, what is really cool is being able to understand that a big change is going on and realizing that this shift
takes time. If anything, if you're gay, you should be pretty excited
that you're living in a time where you can witness this shift. I
mean, acceptance of homosexuality is perhaps the biggest "game-
changer" since the civil rights movement. And before that, the
dawning notion that rape was not a good thing. And before that,
the wheel. And fire. And Joan Rivers's first face-lift.

Sexual behavior, to me, is no cooler than eating. Declaring your sexual freedom—gay or straight—is akin to declaring your ability to eat forty-five hot dogs in a minute. (On a particular block in Midtown Manhattan, very akin. As in, the same.) Straight men who cannot stop talking about their conquests are no different from a gay activist's jockstrap dance during a parade. It falls under one heading in my mind: "So what?" Choosing to be defined by who you sleep with seems about as uncool as being defined by your low-carb diet. It's why I shut up about my bacon and mayonnaise intake (it was hurting the ratings). I dislike gays, straights, blacks, Hispanics, Jews, all people in fact, if their identity means more to them than their achievements.

But forget gays. They should be vocal about gay marriage. (Even if some really don't want it. That's part of marriage too—wanting it, and not wanting it, but still having the choice.) I'm more irritated by straights who go out of their way to announce their allegiance to an issue, simply as a way to distance themselves from the Neanderthals who've not yet evolved. I'm fairly certain that many of them made their decision based on the need to appeal to the cooler crowd. I've seen it myself: The self-satisfaction of a person announcing he is for gay marriage approaches the same sensation experienced when someone says, "I don't eat veal," or, "I would never buy anything at Walmart." It's an announcement masked as achievement, and it's as boring as an Oscar acceptance speech. And about as substantial as a campaign promise.

Last week, I was sitting outside at my favorite Italian restaurant on Ninth Avenue. A chap on a date sat next to me and began telling me what he did for "a living." I put "a living" in quotes because I don't consider what he did an actual job. He and some other activists had rented or purchased a house across from the Westboro Baptist Church in Topeka, Kansas, with the express purpose of confronting them over their virulent antigay views.

It's a funny story, until I asked him how many members are in this crazy church. Maybe fifty, he said. We had this discussion, mind you, a week after the Boston bombing. So I asked, "Would you ever do this to a mosque?" He looked at me silently, but he knew the answer. Of course he'd never confront the homophobia of Islam, because it's not as cool as doing it to crazy old white folks. Confronting Muslims over their bigotry could be construed as Islamophobia, and really, it's just safer to stick to the whiteys in Topeka. They won't chop off your head when they're offended. I asked the guy how much press he'd received. His eyes lit up. That's what it was about. I felt sorry for his date. I think she picked up the check.

My advice: Remaining calm and understanding in regard to different views on sexuality may not make you any cooler, but it might make you a tad more compassionate. Primarily toward those folks who, while holding no animosity toward gays, feel threatened by gay marriage.

Recently an ESPN analyst was barbecued on Twitter for speaking his mind about NBA player Jason Collins revealing that he was gay. Chris Broussard said plainly: "If you're openly living that type of lifestyle, then the Bible says, 'You know them by their fruits,' it says that that's a sin." And "If you're openly living in unrepentant sin, whatever it may be, not just homosexuality—adultery, fornication, premarital sex between heterosexuals, whatever it may be—I believe that's walking in open rebellion to God and Jesus Christ, so I would not characterize that person as a Christian."

Before you call him a homophobe, recognize that his view, however wrong, is steeped in religious belief. And he lumped straights into the whole sinful mess. You can belittle him all you want, but it won't help you understand him any better. Had you wanted to. And you should.

The same applies to Phil Robertson from *Duck Dynasty*. Fact is, his beliefs on gays do not include anything about taking action. He has views on sin, but his opinions won't hurt you.

Last, all of this preoccupation with who's gay and who isn't (actually, no one cares about who *isn't* gay) falls under one mistake the cool make: making sexuality important at an age when other things matter more. I get the importance of dealing with sexual confusion and the jerks who bully those who seem different. But making the assertion of one's sexuality an achievement (one that needs to be reiterated through constant practice) goes absolutely nowhere. Civilization's recent predicament with modern sexuality—that it is cool to celebrate it without pondering its consequences—has left us with hordes of miserable single people. It has left us with fatherless kids. It has left us with rampant STDs—some extremely distressing strains that continue to morph as we try to screw our way past them. I hope gay marriage helps tamp down these scary stats. But really, it doesn't matter to me whether you are gay or straight. What's uncool is assuming we care.

THE REBEL BOOTLICKER

Why would anyone not be a liberal? Think of the rewards! You're an eternal teenager, always in sync with the cool kids, never a target of scowls, a consistent beneficiary of invites to events involving lamb sliders, crab cake tacos, and desperate come-ons from Adrian Grenier. You secretly feel superior to all those around you who have yet to evolve. You get to pronounce "Pakistan" as "pock-ist-aahn." You become an international walking guidebook for pretentious pronunciation. But you're as rebellious as a seat cushion.

The public acquiescence to liberal ideas has flourished for decades, unquestioned and unfettered, solely because of the cool assumption that leftism is rebellious. Given that for the left, dissent is not tolerated, this makes no sense. You can't be a rebel *and* a sheep. It's not possible. I remember Andrew Breitbart telling me a story about being at a posh party in Aspen, where he was having a friendly conversation with the wealthy host. They were getting along fine, and the host graciously offered Andrew and his wife an invitation to come stay with them over a weekend, perhaps to ski. Maybe an hour later, the host's wife found out Breit-bart's political leanings and confronted Andrew, informing him that the invitation was rescinded. How petty, but also, how pre-dictable. God bless Andrew's wife, who was no firebrand like AB but had to reap the consequences his beliefs wrought. Their road was bumpier than a Klingon's forehead.

The problem with this free intellectual ride given to the left—it allows really stupid people to pull it off. There are tons of libs who are smart, but there are far more who are stupid. Yet they realize that simply saying the "right" thing creates an illusion of intelligence. If all you have to really do is denigrate the mono-lithic evil that is America, or the corrupt machine that is capi-talism, or the ruthless single-minded viciousness of our military, you can pretty much turn off your brain. All that stuff has been said before, to be sure, usually by someone considered a great thinker by the intelligentsia. And all of it easily translates into shorthand that helps conquer every kind of cocktail party sce-nario. Just say, "A little socialism never hurt anybody" on either coast and you're in the club. Even if you couldn't spell "socialism" with a dictionary on hand and a crossbow to your head.

You see this a lot with pop stars who inevitably fear that they are as shallow as a tambourine. After spending their younger years consuming and consumed by ego, they suddenly realize that there is a way to rise above the lightweight reputation that comes with being young, rich, and vacuous. So they embrace liberal causes to appear deep. I call it the "Madonna syndrome," although she wasn't the first to discover it. But it's since been adopted by everyone from Lady Gaga to that aging gasbag Jon Bon Jovi. Their discovery of "politics" is a breathless embrace of left-wing clichés, often expressed in cringe-producing interviews and horrendously adolescent tweets. Watching a celebrity talk politics is like watching a politician sing. There are exceptions. Like Bono, who as he ages seems to salute the machinery of capitalism that made him wealthy. In mixed company no less. But his social conscience couldn't be better established if he were Bishop Tutu doing an anti-fracking interpretive dance. With Tina Fey. On an Indian reservation.

I'd say look at Cher as an example and her increasingly unhinged attacks on the right, but I would never suggest anyone "look at Cher." I would say "look at the human being formally known as Cher. She is officially a cyborg." So read her tweets instead. She's now prone to intolerant, vicious attacks on those who think differently from her.

This was her recent take on Senator Ted Cruz:

> I love crazies who crawl out from under Rocks to
> defend a scumbag who is beneath contempt! He
> makes Joe McCarthy seem like Mother Teresa!

There are more, many of them targeted at the usual suspects: gun owners, Walmart, Tea Partiers, Republicans. This is the poor crone's road back to relevance, and who can blame her? She's too old to do *Dancing with the Stars*. Twitter is where old cranks go to live and to die; and it's exactly how they would want to die—with an audience cheering on their every last crackpot thought. (Note to my relatives: The moment I hit sixty, kill my Twitter account. I fear I may end up tweeting about my Pat Sajak fantasies—and I prefer to keep all that stuff for my memoirs.)

The bedrock of cool politics is simple: Help everyone into the warm, fuzzy arms of government. It's not exactly a horrible thing to believe, if you close your eyes to the unintended (or perhaps intended) consequences. In order for this cool idea to survive unscathed, you have to ignore history and detach the incompetence from the price paid by taxpayers. As a kid, I had no idea where things came from. I didn't realize we paid for the stuff we got. Dad made 25K a year, but he could have been a millionaire. When the milk arrived, I saw the milk (and the milkman, because I'm that old) but never the bill. This is the brain of the child and the liberal. There's a wall between candy and its cost.

So the belief that government is a good thing that you work for (as opposed to the other way around, the government being awful and it works for you) puts cool kids at an advantage. Because there is no shortage of ideas when the answer is always yes. If a solution to one troubled program is another troubled program, then you can always be Santa Claus. You can keep saying yes, as long as the connection between benefit and cost is never made. You can do this till the day you die, where you'll be eulogized by a drum circle of IRS agents.

So when a TV host asks a conservative guest, "What can the government do about health care?," the answer "nothing but harm" may be true, but it's also uncool and mean. If government is a board game, the right comes off like a petulant child refusing to roll the dice. Government is the game, and we're the pissy kid who won't play. Asking a conservative for "government solutions to a problem" is like asking a surgeon to name his favorite cancer. Asking a libertarian to nominate their favorite government program is like asking a hemophiliac to name his favorite sharp object.

Which is why the left is always portrayed as the cool cat, offering solutions that make poor people smile, while the right-winger comes off as cold and brutal, as he shakes his head dismissively, rejecting such romantic wrongheaded notions. Never mind that the solutions offered are abstract poisons, and poisons that

kill you slowly. By not offering government-administered alterna-
tives, we are uncool. Until libertarians offer their own form of
"government program," they will always be seen as aloof, heart-
less, and evil.

Here's what I call the Stossel experiment.

Imagine John Stossel, a good-looking chap, taking a pill that
would have him say, "We really need more programs to feed the
poor and help the homeless." That Stossel would be a movie star.

Now imagine Stossel saying, "We need government to stop
helping the poor because the more they help, the more they
hurt." That Stossel would have a weekly show on Fox Business.

Life would be more glamorous for Stossel if he took the damn
pill.

Where does a nation end up, under the thumb of the cool?
You have a welfare state mired in debt with nothing to show for
it. It's a three-pronged attack on everything that made America
the greatest country ever, a combination of incompetence, a deg-
radation of society's desire to create and grow, and an economy
that simply cannot keep up.

It's strange to me that the cool, by their very definition committed to being against "the Man," would embrace an endless
maze of bureaucracies that turns everyone into passive zombies,
waiting for their allotment of bread and cheese. In the name of
the public good, the cool happily hand over their power of individual freedom and the dynamic economy that it produces to a
bloated blob of arbitrary administration. You have the media-
academic complex saluting protesters demanding more government, so they can do—and think—less. They are marching in
favor of dependency. They are marching for the right to suck.

The secret principle governing the cool is a belief that human
beings have no imagination, no creativity, no ability to achieve.

Without the centralized beast to hold us together, providing us with the most mediocre of product, we would suffer. The lie, of course, is that the cool is exempt from its own assumptions. They don't need the government to tell them what to do, whether it be stop drinking sodas or sock away money for retirement, but it must work for everyone else. And that's the reason the cool push this nonsense—for them the consequences are divorced from cost. As millions of Americans suffer from horrible decisions they promoted (like Obamacare), they can move merrily along, to the next cause that strikes their fancy. Without ever bothering to follow up on the results of their championed causes, they continue to push even more destructive ideas on those less fortunate. A cool cat can argue vehemently for gun control, for he lives safe and secure in a benign community. It's the bodega owner left unarmed who has to worry. The media can trumpet the notion of universal health care. Then, when it's in place, the media isn't present to catalog its horrors. The media screws you, then when the baby is born, it leaves town on the first bus. With your last twenty bucks. Without a backward glance or a hint of guilt.

And that's the scariest part of the cool's promotion of government—it's their chosen form of relationship, and it can only be fulfilled through dependence. Perhaps in their own lives, they found their own personal relationships wanting, and see government as an ideal replacement. I'm not sure. What I do know is that when you offer the option of government as Daddy, it robs the community of actual daddies. It robs us of the initial human response, which is to solve these problems among ourselves, first. Here's what I know in my life: If someone offers to do something for me, I let them do it. When the government now acts as proxy for community (wasn't it the Obama 2012 campaign that said that government is what we all had in common?), what's the point of community? Especially when the efforts made by a community to sustain itself are so firmly blocked by a restless, carnivorous bureaucracy always looking for another way in, and larger and larger pension benefits. People telling us how much we need government—they are always the people in government!

The media has spent decades making a mockery of religion, and I get why. It's easy. Religious people can lack irony, and they often appear humorless and credulous. If you need a piñata for a skit or a late-night joke, there's a bag of embarrassing televangelists and disgraced holy men to choose from. But there's another reason for the constant belittlement. The media sees religion as competition to government, and government, these days, is just media with a military. They are all the same people: the media, the government, academia. They are all populated by a cool clique that advocates expansion of their influence as a solution to our problems. Government, the *New York Times*, Harvard, it's all from the same vat of shysters who think they're better than you.

You can laugh at religion all you want. As a troubled agnostic, I'm not the best-equipped defender. But for years religion in a community setting grounded us and helped foster a caring collectivism (as opposed to economic collectivism) that actually worked. The church made obligations obvious; the recipients felt it immediately. They saw the cost, and they felt the results. It also got you out of the house on Sunday. Not a small thing, especially during football season.

When government intrudes, community is replaced by entitlement and everyone gets in line, not just the folks who need it most. My guess is that a lot of the forty-plus million on food stamps need it, and a lot of them don't. But it doesn't matter; if it's there to be taken, why not take it? And as a member of a community, what's required of you now? Not much. Show up, get in line, take the handout. It used to be called Sovietization. Now it's called progressive policy. And very, very few people ever voluntarily give it up.

Let's face it, people, the more we rely on government, the less we rely on ourselves. We've seen the collapse of family life. Two-parent households are dwindling rapidly. No one sticks around. And the safety net did its job; it made it that much easier to stomach an economic collapse. Hooray. Is it a coincidence that cities implode as government expands? Is it any wonder that as government expands, illegitimacy soars? Is it any wonder that as government expands, the poor stay poor? Unchecked government is a vast, ever-expanding monster (and not nearly as sexy as Mothra).

If you explained this to the cool, that their infatuation with government is actually harmful, even deadly, would they listen? Not on your life. Because it's uncool not to believe in government. If there's a hole in your life, you need to fill it with stuff. The government has stuff. Make the government give more stuff. Never mind that free stuff does nothing to encourage achievement or gain any kind of moral wisdom. It does the opposite. Do a search of lottery winners. The more you give to someone, the worse it gets.

Meanwhile, the cool question, mock, and deride the things that actually work. Think about capitalism, which has done more for humanity than exercise, alcohol, and kitten videos combined. Somehow, the coolies who favor a one-size-fits-all, soulless government are the same ones who think capitalism dehumanizes people. They will say that not everyone has access to capitalism, but they all have access to government. It's as though they skipped that integral step that makes life worth living. Something called "effort." Capitalism works if you apply effort. And, to quote some comic I can't remember: If you can't make it here, you can't make it anywhere. America is the easiest place on the planet to make a buck. Look at me for crying out loud. I'd be a fire hydrant anywhere else. (And I'd like it.)

I'm not against welfare programs, I'm just against a welfare state. There is a difference. It's like ice cream. It's not a bad thing a few times a week, but try eating it every day. You are what you eat and the welfare state is the worst ice cream there is. Worse than Indian pudding.

The cool push a way of life that only they can afford. As with the rock star who can do all the drugs he wants, it's the groupies he did the drugs with that need to find a way home the next day as the rock star hops on his jet. Society lives in the wake of cool's destructive policies.

The American decline, which coincides with an ascendant government, is not the cool's problem. It's ours. And the only way to beat it is to beat them. Perhaps with a stick. Or something like a stick. I'll leave that choice up to you. That's what libertarians do.

THE RISE OF THE
FREE RADICAL

So why do the cool prosper when they suck so bad? More important, how can we realign the universe so that the things that are really cool (i.e., what isn't cool now) take precedence over the crap spawned by the coolerati?

We need to redefine cool as "what allows you to do the things you want to do with the people you love and care about." In America's wildly successful epoch, that's been hard work, decent moral values, a viciously badass military, a no-bullshit analysis of the world around us, and a desire to understand the world without the assistance of style editors and root-cause experts. Our current idolization of short talk show hosts has also yielded global dividends.

So who are the truly cool? The truly cool are those who achieve greatness without giving a second thought to impressing others. It's about doing things for the right reasons, usually unnoticed. True cool, in my book, is something that's uniquely, and surprisingly, good. The elements that make up this murky nonspecific goodness include, but are not limited to:

▸ **Honesty.** You cannot be a liar, or a phony, and be cool. That's why so many people who are described as cool often aren't. Ever see a picture of a "cool actor" from before they were famous? Goofballs in scarves. That's who they really are. Everything else is a lie. Simply put: If you have to try really hard to convince us, you've already lost.

▸ **Fidelity to principle.** It's somebody who sticks to his guns, and is considered brave, in the course of daily events. He has a spine and it's a pretty obvious one.

▸ **Unpredictability that starts to make sense once you realize the person has a code.** Remember when you first met someone and thought, "Wow, this person is odd. Why is he doing that?" Then over time, you find that his behavior isn't erratic at all, that there is an internal consistency embedded in his behavior that explains every tic. Andrew Breitbart is the key example. If you didn't know him, you thought he was bonkers. Once you became friends, every action was part of a complete point of view that made wonderful, perfect sense, and even explained his wildly esoteric "contacts" list.

▸ **Persuasive correctness.** It is one thing to be right, but it takes a real character to be right and explain why in simple, straightforward terms. And this sense of "rightness" transcends the left/right duopoly. It's what makes the cool person a benefit to the country. Christ—we need more of these.

The people who fit these criteria I call the Free Radicals. They embody these qualities, rebel against rebellion, are cool without being dishonest, and do what they know is right, even if it makes them look out of step. But they're not. They're the most interesting people we've got. The Free Radicals I admire are:

Black conservatives: It's not about black skin, it's about thick skin. They could go one way and never face scorn. But instead they follow their brains and their hearts. They earn the scorn of white liberals, who hate them for pissing on their worldview, and the enmity of black liberals, who see them as traitors. God bless 'em and watch over them. They need it.

Dana Perino. Seriously, answer this question: How does a ninety-pound farm girl get herself into the White House? And handle it with such ease? I'd say more but it might give her a bigger head, and she'd probably fall over. She's already a human lollipop as is.

Australia and New Zealand. Australia is pretty much America in the 1950s with better-looking women and uglier insects. I'm pretty sure they've fought alongside America in every conflict since World War I. Both Australia and New Zealand are frontiers, a few generations from a penal colony past, living on China's lip, and still willing to say, "Go fuck yourself." They are the great hidden bulwark against future threats. Think about it: If you were uncontrollable, England sent you to Australia. If you were uncontrollable there, Australia sent you to New Zealand. Deal with that, China.

Reason **magazine.** The smartest magazine around. You want proof? Both me and Breitbart applied for jobs there, and both of us were turned down. I hold no grudges.

The New York Police Department. You gotta wonder why Chicago has more homicides with one-third the people (which destroys the "New York's reduction in crime is emblematic of the whole country" theory). These guys and gals, roughly 50 percent of whom are minorities, have ignored mountains of media criticism, while lowering crime 90 percent in twelve years. I'd say that 80 percent of the lives they saved are minorities. So while all those gripes from the left's fever swamps continue to vomit forth, the NYPD continues to save more black and Hispanic babies. Yet, at Bill de Blasio's inauguration, the chaplain for the Sanitation Department called the city a "plantation." It's over, people, when the chaplain for the Sanitation Department is taken seriously.

Ambassador John Bolton. Thick glasses? Check. Goofy grin? Yep. A walrus mustache? Absolutely. The uncoolest guy on the planet, yet the only one willing to stand up to our planet's tyrants. If President Obama had just 10 percent of the Bolton gene, I wouldn't be worried most of my life.

Bjørn Lomborg. He's an environmentalist who strays from the bunch by being rational, thoughtful, and resistant to panic. He believes in global warming (a "lukewarmer," if you will) but also knows the facts: that there are way worse threats out there, and by obsessing over the marginal consequences of global warming, greenies ignore threats that kill millions more poor people across the world. Plus, his name is Bjørn, and he's not in ABBA.

Killer whales. The coolest animal. They are not a fish, they are air-breathing, and they eat endangered species (polar bears). They remind me of me, with slightly better breath.

Fracking. It's not a person but a thing, and it's a thing that's driving environmentalists nuts. It's actually "cleaner" energy (there is no such thing as "clean energy"—unless you count Adderall), and it's robustly reviving economies in states across the country. It's killing the left from two angles: They hate industry and despise anything that isn't a renewable resource. Fracking is their Antichrist. And my hero. It will help America survive the twenty-first century while Europe slides back into the nineteenth century.

Straight couples. Right now they're about as boring and uncool as a bread machine. But what makes them cool? They make gay people. Seriously, without straight couples, we'd have absolutely no gay people whatsoever. Well, we'd have *no* people whatsoever. So thank them for the human race.

The overweight and out-of-shape. Clearly they're busy with something else. And that's the real reason why incredibly fit people are really uncool. If you can work out for hours a day and not be a pro athlete, then you're running from something. I'm talking about me. As a jack-ass who worked out between two and three hours a day for at least a decade, I stopped when I discovered what a tool I'd been. I'm still a tool, but I'm a fat one, and I'm doing something with my life. Which is what a lot of fat, out-of-shape people are busy doing too. Look at Winston Churchill. Would you rather have that fat asshole or a trimmer Adolf Hitler, the vegetarian? No need to answer (I can't hear you).

Smokers. I don't put this on the list because smoking happens to look cool (it does, if you happen to be handsome);

it's here because I do it. How much longer is anyone's guess. I smoke no more than five cigs a day. If you think there's something wrong with that, I'm willing to be wrong in your mind. Imbibing five of anything is only bad if whatever it is happens to be bigger than your fist.

Broads. Not women. Broads. Brassy drinkers who swear and shoot from the hip and the lip. My favorite broad at the moment is Elizabeth MacDonald, a Fox Business news contributor. I'd like to share a bottle of Jack with her. And then go shoot things. Perhaps named Jack.

Waiting tables. Note: I didn't say waiters, because for every good waiter you get, there's one who deserves to have his fingernails removed. But restaurant work is a must in any background. You blog? In the john? Who cares? Get out and wash dishes. It's good for the soul. And you can stop and never do it again when you're done.

The military. It's the last place on earth to be poisoned by the toxins of political correctness. Which is why it's the only branch of government that works. Every veteran I've worked with is a total pro. It is true that showing up is 90 percent of life, but showing up *on time* is 100 percent. I suppose when you spend the past few years being shot at, I'm not that intimidating a sight to see in a control room. When I complain about the lighting, they give me a look that says, "How'd you'd like to see a latrine, head first?"

Ramirez. In the world of political cartooning, not being a liberal makes you a leper. This guy is the Hispanic political cartoonist who happens to be staunchly conservative—

about as common as a flying wildebeest. It's easy to be a leftist with a crayon. All you have to do is draw a cloud and write REPUBLICAN BIGOTRY in it, and then sketch a kitten below it, with the words OUR NATION'S CHILDREN across it. Ramirez is way more talented than his peers, and he has to be, or they'd already have drummed him out of the profession. He draws better than all of them, which must really irk Garry Trudeau. (But everything irks Garry Trudeau. Primarily, one suspects, Garry Trudeau.)

Hirsi Ali. She may be a woman, but she has more balls than a McDonald's play pit. An outspoken critic of Muslim abuses toward women, Ayaan Hirsi Ali (she wrote the script for Theo van Gogh's movie *Submission*, which ultimately led to his murder by Muslim supremacists) is targeted by hate groups, including al-Qaeda, who put her on its most recent hit list. They all want to kill her, and they very well may. But it doesn't stop her. Balls. Luckily she can count on the left and women's groups for support. If by support you mean disinterest.

Iranian metal bands and Persian ravers. In America, if you want quick cool cachet, just get into music. Learn an instrument, grow your hair long, and join a band. Or if you're lazy, just become a modern deejay—you'll probably still get laid. But try doing all of that in countries where the added edge is that you could die for singing. There's something wonderful about kids going out and doing something totally ridiculous, disposable, and fun—when they know it could cost them their lives. All Western kids risk is STD. These kids risk being DOA.

Fossil fuels. Talk about the ultimate recycling: We are running our planes, trains, and automobiles on dead dinosaurs. Christ, how can you *not* love that idea? It still blows my mind that it's possible (the same way I guess that Insane Clown Posse were transfixed by magnets), and I find it insanely hypocritical that environmentalists reject this truly renewable fuel (true, it's only renewed once, but that's a start). Thanks, dinosaur fossils—you may never know how many people you've helped by being dead. The world essentially runs on Apatosaurus farts. And we're supposed to be ashamed of that?

Japan. I'm pretty sure it's the size of Connecticut, but it acts like it has the power of Texas. Which it does. This place stands up to China more than the hall monitor in the White House. The only reason they don't openly mock us for our weakness is that they're just too damn polite. Plus, they all know karate. I saw it in a movie.

Professional wrestling. Fake violence is actually way better than real violence. It's true. These are male soap operas, or "anglo novellas," where you can look at sweaty muscular men in tights and not worry about your website browsing history.

Legal immigrants. These are the guys who didn't cut the line. The ones who waited. Come on in and have a seat. You deserve it. Sorry we treat you worse than your illegal brethren. We're a confused nation!

A snub nose .38. It's what you call a "force multiplier," as noted in *Taxi Driver*. It fits in your sock, but don't put it there—that's illegal. (Plus, you'll get blisters!) It's really snug in all legal, commercial holsters. It never jams. Best part: one or two .38 rounds will still a rapist's ambition, guaranteed. The best friend that a woman, a gay, a minority businessman in a rough neighborhood could ever have, even if liberal mayors hate them (as they're surrounded by a bevy of packing behemoths).

Truman Capote. A five-foot-two chubby gay fights his way out of the South and writes *In Cold Blood.* A fantastic controller of language who seemed bemused by his own orientation. Probably one of the most interesting conservatives America has ever produced. The size of a college fridge, he took a world of shit for never giving in and becoming a lefty so Gore Vidal might like him. Of Jack Kerouac—the writer who spills off the lips of wannabe cool kids when asked who they read—Capote said, "That's not writing, that's typing." Sort of a gay male Dana Perino. Maybe a little taller.

Governor Mike Huckabee. Kinda funny that a Southern hillbilly Bible thumper now thumps bass with all these rock legends. Watching him *thunka-thunk* that bass, in his suit, to me is priceless. Plus he lets me take the leftovers from his green room. The food, I mean.

Monks. I lived in a monastery for a week, and you can't walk away from that with the intent of making the whole experience sound precious. It wasn't. It was brutally boring. I cannot live without input from people, electronics, alcohol. The monks are a different sort. It's not that they don't care; they just don't care for *stuff.* They are proof that you can live in the sixteenth century without demanding that everyone else do the same. Certain religions can take a page from that. Not that I'm naming any, of course.

Old ladies. They're not always wrinkled totems of wisdom. Some can be a pain in the ass. Especially the one who used to live downstairs from me who took up the bassoon. I just like old ladies because they made it this far. They deserve the planet's attendance award. This is an unforgiving hell, and it never ever gets better. How they know that, and still press on, gives hope to misanthropes like myself.

Mark E. Smith. He's the lead singer of the long-running psycho-rock band the Fall. Nearly every record bristles with repetitive originality, and an insanity that comes from one place—Mark. But I became a lifelong fan when I came across an interview he did where the music journalist pressed him on his politics and why he tended to abhor the liberalism that other bands embrace. Smith's accent is thick, but I remember the gist of this response. "Why don't terrorists bomb colleges? Because they'd kill their mates." He made the simple link between the pernicious romance with fascism you find among intellectuals, and terror—something other pop singers and musicians never do. That's cool. And smart. I can almost forgive him for using his middle initial.

1950s sports figures. They were so much cooler because they just came and played. Compare a Willie Mays to a bum like Barry Bonds. Yes, I have a personal vendetta against Bonds—he used to sit behind me in Spanish class in high school and kick my chair for answers to quizzes, but I'd feel the same about the schmuck regardless. Back then playing sports was just enough. You didn't need to own a nightclub or have a fleet of cars or showcase your tacky house on horrible television shows. You just did your thing and thanked God that you did something way more fun than any other thing you could be doing. Plus, they rarely got arrested. At least not for murder.

My wife. She is here, of course, to keep me in good spirits. But we met in Portugal, we lived in London, and she came to America from Moscow and worked her butt off. She's the ultimate immigrant, one who stood in line, filled out the forms, and didn't complain. She also embraces America's free markets and potential for achievement, perhaps because she came from a place that had none of that. By the way, I should put all Russians alongside her—at least the ones I've met. They're more capitalist than the capitalists who are born here, and they have no illusions about socialism. Don't mess with them. There's a reason the Wehrmacht got only as far as Stalingrad.

Frank Miller. Talk about a mysterious anomaly, Frank's a right-wing comic book geek from my neighborhood. He sketches all sorts of horrific realities, unafraid to call out the real terror in the world. As other artists bend over backward to incorporate politically correct themes in their work, he bends forward into an area that makes his peers uncomfortable. He's a fearless sort, which is why there are so few like him. Plus, his use of black in his panels changed how comics and its movie genre look. Let's see a left-wing twerp like Ted Rall do that.

Joe Escalante. He's not just a bass player for the Vandals; he's also a part-time judge, a lawyer, a member of a Smiths tribute band, and, of all things, a do-it-yourself bullfighter. A deeply rooted Catholic and an unapologetic pro-lifer, he makes the description "punk rocker" richer for it. He is truly punk, for he punks all the tame posers around him, simply by showing up. He's a Renaissance man, but you'd never know it by talking to him. A true Renaissance hombre.

The *South Park* guys. They could start a movement if they wanted to. But instead, they convey moral messages through their work that no one would touch. Sure, they poke fun at Mormonism, but they also make fun of the religions that might kill you—and they've paid for that. Hell, their work resulted in a terror plot in Times Square. When you inspire that, you know you're doing the right thing. I just wish I could remember their names.

Mike Judge. If you don't believe that Beavis and Butt-head were the sages of a generation, then you were not listening. Crude, primitive, and simple, Judge's creations helped expose a vacuous culture consumed by cool. But his crowning achievement might in fact be the movie *Idiocracy*, which chillingly predicts where an obsession with material cool ends up. In the film, which came and went faster than a skittish cockroach, Judge attacks the death of thinking. He envisioned a future where society brutalizes anyone who ventures a coherent thought. Essentially, America two years from now. It's hilarious and harrowing, and it sticks with you whenever you happen to find yourself roaming a mall, quietly wishing you were dead.

Margaret Thatcher. A gray-haired, middle-aged woman who rocked the world, and even scared Reagan a bit. She had so much spine inside her, she was able to lend it to other leaders of the free world. I never saw the movie about her because I find Meryl Streep to be a poor man's Stella Stevens.

Gavin McInnes. As a young, scummy Scottish-Canadian punk, he founded a lurid piece of trash called *Vice*, a magazine that soon grew to a massive worldwide brand. Sure, his look (beard, tattoos, trucker hats) has been copied by every ad agency to make a buck. Underneath it all is a deeply religious family man who realized that true rebellion is a rebellion against the cool's predictable assumptions. He is still vile, rude, unpredictable, and at times a full-on asshole. But he's also a rare breed: an honest, fearless jerk. And funnier than 99 percent of the comedians who call themselves comedians.

John Yoo. Vilified by the left for authoring papers legally justifying the use of torture, he's never backed down in reaction to his detractors. To this day, he still makes a cohesive argument as to why his stance will save America from its enemies. You can hate him all you want, but every foreign policy success President Obama can claim (which is perhaps one—the capture and killing of Osama bin Laden) can be traced back to Yoo. He also came out strongly against the lenient sentence received by that traitorous scum Bradley Manning. His Harvard cocktail party days are over. I'm sure he couldn't give a shit. He's the lawyer Obama wishes he was.

Fred Armisen. If you only know him from his tame, paltry impressions of Obama on *Saturday Night Live*, you're missing something. His IFC show, *Portlandia*, is a gentle thumb in the eye of all progressives. But his work rises above stereotypical condemnations because hipsters are his people. Only a person in tune with the naive left could create such a magnificent parody of the lifestyle. When you watch *Portlandia*, you realize that he actually loves the people he mocks. And that's instructive, at least for me, a jerk who is quick to dismiss such folks as predictable, narrow-minded fools. It's nice to see that even if I can't stand some people, they're still people. Well, barely.

Penn Jillette. One half of Penn and Teller, he might be the free-est radical of them all, a nondrinking, nondrugging atheist genius who operates without a mean bone in his body. He inspired this book, somehow. I owe him for allowing me the privilege of his friendship. I just hope he never falls on me.

Ben Carson. A black conservative doctor who pisses the hell out of the left because he is a black conservative doctor. He may be soft-spoken, but his words weigh heavy on the mind. I'd fake a seizure just so I could get an appointment to talk to him.

Lupe Fiasco. A gifted mind with a gift for language, he spends his Sundays on Twitter, posing philosophical questions that evade most pop star minds. He's genuinely interested in the world around him rather than how the world fits around him. He says things that anger his fans and confuse his critics. He's a human Rubik's Cube that very few, if anyone, actually solve.

Roger Ailes. He's not in here because he's my boss. He's in here because he suffers for his work. And refuses to waver. The more you attack, the more he presses on. Vitriol from adversaries becomes a fuel—the mark of a true rebel, and one who understands the fragility of freedom more than most of his critics are willing to admit.

Andy Levy. Perhaps the strangest normal person you might meet, or the most normal oddball you might meet. Either way, I can almost never predict what might come out of his mouth at any given time. Which keeps me on my toes and pushes me to work harder at being clever, when the alternative—kicking back and accepting certain assumptions about the world—would have been far easier.

Andrew WK. A creator of relentlessly positive, addictive music, he is a one-man Queen, with the ego of a pine nut. Anyone who has worked with Andrew knows this: He enters every adventure with the energy of a dervish and the good-natured sensibility of a care-free Eagle Scout. Built within his party ethos is a singular desire to bring joy to this earth, which he does wherever he goes. I never know what he's thinking, perhaps because he's eight steps ahead of me at all times.

Skunk Baxter. A guitarist for two seminal bands from the 1970s—Steely Dan and the Doobie Brothers—and a star on one particularly classic episode of *What's Happening!!* (the one about bootlegging), he's also an expert in missile defense systems. Self-taught, he wrote a paper on how to convert ship-based anti-aircraft missiles into some sort of defense system (he explained this to me at a bar, three times, and it still didn't absorb), which landed him on the Civilian Advisory Board for Ballistic Missile Defense. He roams the Pentagon and consults with the intel community and is so frighteningly smart I wonder if he has three brains instead of one. Amazingly, all of his ideas about fighting terror came from his music past. He's also a sheriff and carries a gun in a fanny pack. When he tells you why, it makes so much sense that I went out and bought a fanny pack.

King Buzzo. The guitarist for perhaps the most unpredictable metal band in history, The Melvins, he is responsible for the heaviest music this side of Pluto. I've yet to understand the lyrics to any of the songs—songs, mind you, that I've listened to thousands of times. He could have been content to create structured, easy-to-follow hard rock, but that's not his style. He makes devious metal, the kind that hints at awesomeness, because hitting you over the head with it would be too easy. He's wicked smart, a ball of mirth, and truly open-minded. But he's open-minded in a way that scares those who only pretend to be. His brain makes me nervous, as his guitar playing makes me shiver. "Honeybucket" remains the best heavy metal song ever, and maybe my favorite song of all time.

Tom Fec. Also known as Tobacco, Fec fronts Black Moth Super Rainbow, the first real electronic answer to heavy metal. He may not even be aware of it, but he somehow is able to create the heaviest music on the planet using the lightest of instruments. "Maniac Meat" will go down as a record so far ahead of its time that as newer bands emulate it they will get the credit reserved for him—and only him. He is shy to a fault, and the moment he decides to own his place in music, he will be bigger than those who command the spotlight now. I am fairly certain he doesn't worry about such things, but that's what obsessive fans like me are for.

Torche. This band is cool because it defies categorization. You can call it metal. Or doom. Or pop. All I know is, its members are so immensely talented, and so pure in conviction, that they are the closest in approximating early U2's promise. It would be a crime if they aren't owning arenas in eighteen months. Their music demands a producer that sees this promise and desires to treat them like the arena band they already are, even if they don't see it themselves.

Ginger Wildheart. A furious workaholic who creates riff-laden gems at the pace of a maniacal chord-bending conveyor belt, Ginger was one of the first artists to drag his fans along with him into the new world. Seeing the world change, and possibilities for survival dwindle in the traditional musical environment, he's now on the forefront of a new kind of movement: a musical concierge who creates songs especially for those who love them.

Billy Zoom. The coolest looking guitarist in history, minus the pretensions that come from being the coolest looking guitarist in history. Taciturn, calm, and agreeable, he unleashes riffs effortlessly—as a member of X—and outcools peers who feel the need to express themselves in ways that merit, at best, a shrug. He's the Clint Eastwood of guitar slingers—everyone else, by comparison, are Matt Damons.

Devin Townsend. A gentle genius with a bottomless voice and a vicious guitar. If you come across one of his fans and see the manic devotion in their eye, it's not unwarranted. He's a rarity, the cult leader who never intended to run a cult. But there it is. I would urge you to pick up *Epicloud*. If you don't like it, I would urge you to seek counseling.

Ariel Pink. A purveyor of twisted psychedelic pop, he is as unpredictable as he is smart. Every song is a go-cart raceway of hairpin turns and beautiful melodies that defy interpretation. When I listen to his records, I feel like I discovered a radio station transmitting great pop from a lost city at the bottom of the ocean.

Tom Hazelmyer. Tom might be the only punk rocker who quit a band to join the Marines. And then, after the Marines, he started his own record label, the legendary Amphetamine Reptile. A member of the band Halo of Flies, he's also an insanely talented artist, whose concert posters and album covers are as disturbing as they are appealing. This is how he describes the benefit of joining the military:

> It helped me pull my shit together and focus on what I wanted to do. I doubt that would have happened had I gone the route of my friends from the

neighborhood who wound up being short-order cooks and getting wasted. Nothing like being stranded in a barracks with no money and a guitar to make you knuckle down. It was also helpful in being forced to live and deal with folks from every strata of life, as we all tend to become isolated in our own clique/world. In general, eating a mountain of shit for four years helped keep me grounded and my ego in check when shit was taking off.

I met Tom when King Buzzo brought him along to a *Red Eye* taping. He's a tough mofo, literally. He's the only person I know who survived a coma. The more I read about this guy, the more I realize how much I'd like to be like him. He's about as punk rock a mind you will find, without the pretension of the pretenders.

Gregg Turkington. I came across his alias, the comedian Neil Hamburger, years ago, along with the fearlessness of his antagonistic anti-comedy. I hired him immediately to write for *Maxim* UK. His jokes are pockets of bravery, in that the punch line is often on people who are shocked to find it refutes their expectations. His gag on George Bush is such a brutal prank on the confused audience, it bears telling here:

> "Hey is it just me, is it just me, or is George Bush the worst president in the history of the United States, huh. Am I right?"
> *(The crowd, usually full of young hipsters, would roar with approval after that line.)*

"Which makes it all the harder to understand why his son, George W., is the best president we've had in the United States."

Confused silence would follow that joke. And "Neil" would pause and let the confusion linger. And then he would move on to a joke that merely states the nature of our lives.

"Why does Britney Spears sell so many millions of albums?

"Because the public is horny and depressed."

Felix Dennis. Granted, Felix was my boss for a good part of my career, but he also fired me . . . twice. But I'll be damned if you can find a former crack addict who, in his later stages of life, became one of the best damn poets on the planet. What makes Felix a radical is not the creation of *Maxim* or *Stuff* or *The Week*, it's his poetry. In that realm, he adheres to one particular rule: it must rhyme. And it does so, beautifully. His writing adheres to a discipline, long forgotten, which makes it ultimately rebellious. Years ago, he gave me this poem, for he felt it best summarized my own erratic, bizarre career.

THE FOOL

My friend would ask me, curious,
When we were lads in school,
'You know it makes 'em furious,
Why play the bloody fool?'

My mother she would scold me
Or lecture me in tears;
How many times she told me
To emulate my peers.

When I was one and twenty,
My editor would say:
'You've talent here aplenty,
Why play the fool all day?'

And even my true lover
In gentleness will ask,
'I love you like no other,
Think you I love the mask?'

Their faces set like thunder,
The men with gravitas,
The men whose gold I plunder
Each time I play the ass—

Too late they learn their danger
In breach of fortune's rule,
That Lady Luck's a stranger
To pride, but loves a fool.

That's my list of the coolest people, places, and things on earth. I'm sure I left some out, which makes them even cooler. If I missed them, it's probably because they want to be missed. That's cool.

CONCLUSION: AXING THE
APPETITE FOR ADULATION

The desire to be cool derives from a desire to be liked. But also from a perceived lack of worth. Not being able to accept yourself as "cool" in your own right means you must be deemed cool by someone else who can say, "Yeah, he's cool." A person satisfied with who they are and what they do finds himself inherently resistant to the superficial pulls of the cool. Ideally, I don't need to follow anyone or anything to bolster my ego. The moment you try to persuade me that "early adopters" are now wearing clams on their heads, I will beat the crap out of you with said clams.

It wasn't always like this. As a young kid fresh out of college (back when Heather Locklear was hot), and toiling away at a small magazine in Arlington, Virginia, I found myself ignored and obscured—a twenty-two-year-old in the mailroom watching others get the accolades I felt I deserved (without, of course, ever doing anything for such accolades). This drove me to a mission for acceptance, which ultimately led me to the living room of the world's most successful movie producer (at the time), a man who had just won an Oscar for Best Picture. After flying to Northern

California and purchasing a suit at the local Emporium at San Mateo's Hillsdale Mall (thank you, Mom), and jumping on a flight to LA, I ended up at the doorstep of a famous producer to discuss a screenplay I had only begun to etch out in my scattered, inexperienced brain. Like all young men, I felt that whatever I had to say was meaningful, regardless of the lack of real-world suffering I'd experienced. I talked a lot more than I acted.

I secured the meeting through a college friend whose father was the producer's lawyer. When I showed up that afternoon at a sprawling home somewhere in LA, I was met by a maid of small stature and led into a sunken living room, where I would then wait for "Arnold" to appear shortly (he was bathing, in the after-noon). As I walked into the room, my peripheral vision caught the sight of a servant, holding a tray of drinks. I quickly looked away, as not to awkwardly stare, and took my seat on a couch in front of me. Pretending to ignore him, I could not stop thinking about him. Here I was, with an opportunity to discuss a screenplay with the most powerful man in Hollywood, something I was sure this young man standing behind me had come to LA to do as well. No one comes to LA to become a butler (unless you're British). And here he was standing, having to endure some lucky punk who got a break through a friend. He must have hated my guts. I could feel his stare heating up the back of my neck.

Already a tad nervous, I hated that my one and only opportu-nity to present my dream would be watched by this "someone." It drove me nuts. All I could think about was the butler listening to me, and judging me. Smirking. I knew that, if I were in his shoes, I would do the same thing. I had planned a presentation, but it was evaporating into a mental jumble. I really hated this guy, and I was starting to hate myself, through him.

When Arnold came down, we made some small talk and he

began asking questions. I was already an emotional wreck. I could not focus; my mind was obsessed with the man behind me, assessing my uncool incompetence. This went on for minutes, but it felt like forever. Sensing my desperation, and that something *was* wrong, Arnold got up and said, "You wanna beer?" I said yes, and in time he would bring me a Löwenbräu. Or a Michelob. Either way, it was beer that no longer exists. Maybe I killed it. I don't know. All I know is that I was dying.

After he left to retrieve the lager, I decided that the only way to salvage this disastrous meeting would be to stand up, turn around, and confront the man behind me. He was ruining me. He knew I was a fraud. An impostor. I waited a few moments, and gathered my courage, and stood up.

When I turned around, I found that he was a mannequin, a large dummy holding drinks. He wasn't real. He was a fraud. He was *the* fraud. It reminded me of that feeling you had when you were a kid, at night, in bed, in your dark room, and you swear that you see a monster. You turn on the light, and it's a jacket on a chair. You turn off the light and then minutes later you once again think it's a monster.

Relief and embarrassment came in one big wave. I pulled myself together and sat back down. When Arnold returned, he was greeted by a new me. A better me, who knocked the meeting out of the park. Arnold gave me some encouraging advice and sent me on my merry way. I ended up writing the script. It was horrible, but he convinced me to quit my job and write full-time, which I needed to hear from someone other than my boss at work, who was trying to get rid of me.

The lesson: It is a mistake to worry about how others view you. "Other people" are like images created in your mind. It's only your desire to appease or please or impress them that makes them meaningful. (I refer specifically to peers you wish to impress. Not your family. If they're impressed, you've done your job. And if they're disgusted, you should listen.)

By pretending that the cool are mannequins, you can disarm the desire for cool and eliminate the need for acceptance. You reclaim your authority. You don't need their observation or approval. You're already observed by those who matter: your family, your friends, yourself. Don't let the cool replace those things. Who needs it? You don't. Really, you don't. It won't help you one bit.

We all have the feeling we are being watched, but by what? Our own conscience? Who knows? But we feel it. What we have to learn is that it is better to imagine being watched by something moral and good than by something whose criteria are amoral. Your ego will be fed, but nothing cool will provide that sustenance.

DANKON!

(That's Esperanto for "Thanks!")

The idea for this book grew out of a speech I gave at the Ronald Reagan Presidential Library. I was supposed to be talking about my previous book, *The Joy of Hate* but ended up elaborating on the idea of what is cool and what isn't. I realized that nearly every monologue or segment I've done on my two shows, *The Five* and *Red Eye*, is concerned with one thing that drives me nuts: Why are good things seen as bad, and why are bad things seen as good?

This book answers that question. Or at least tries to. It's all about being cool.

You will find within this book, here and there, bits and pieces of that speech, along with other concepts and ideas I've hit on before in my shows, blogs, and essays. Some of the chapters started out as monologues, throwaway observations on shows, and drunken rants on street corners, and I've expanded on them here, hopefully with a modicum of success. If not, I blame Obama. If he is not impeached by the time this is published, I am leaving the country and moving to Texas.

Dankon!

This is where I thank everyone who helped me, in one way or another, with this book.

First, I thank you for taking the time to read this. It's not a normal book, and I am not a normal person. And most certainly, none of us reading this are seen as cool by those who feel empowered to define the parameters. But we know better.

Of course, I thank Mary Choteborsky, my editor, for poring over this wine-stained manuscript (at this point, it's as crispy as the Dead Sea Scrolls), along with the helpful, energetic staff at Crown, who put up with late-night meetings with a writer who demanded alcohol as a prerequisite for showing up.

I must also thank, in no particular order: Paul Mauro and his lovely wife, Joannie; Aric Webb; my agent Jay Mandel; Roger Ailes (he infused me with confidence—as did all the other wonderful folks at Fox News—but more important, Roger first gave me a chance, meaning he recognized early on that I wasn't normal, and he embraced it); the gang at *The Five*; Andy Levy, Bill Schulz, and the rest of the miscreants who inhabit *Red Eye*; Jack Wright, who has to deal with my butt twice a day; and the loyal pals at Breitbart.com. I thank the ghost of Andrew Breitbart, who may or may not be helping me write this very sentence. Also—thanks to Woody Fraser, who saw the potential early on.

I owe a special thanks to Dana Perino. She is a dear friend, and puts up with my inanities daily, and for that she will be rewarded with two sentences here. I will not mention her dog. (Ah shit, I did.)

People who've inspired this book include a pile of Free Radicals who seem thoroughly uninterested in how they are perceived by the coolerati and would of course not care if they were thanked by me. They are, in no order: Penn Jillette, Andrew W.K., Skunk Baxter, Joe Escalante, Gary Sinise, King Buzzo,

Devin Townsend, Larry Gatlin, Ariel Pink, Gavin McInnes, Ann Coulter, Terry Schappert, Robert Davi, Andrew Elstner, Torche, Tom Fec (a.k.a. Tobacco), Fabio, John Rich, Mike Baker, Jim Norton, Rob Long, Tom Dreeson, Joe DeRosa, Nick DiPaolo, Dirk Benedict, Tom Shillue, Ginger Wildheart, Brandon Belt, Billy Zoom, Gregg Turkington, Tom Hazelmyer, the South. The list continues, perhaps, in the chapter toward the end of the book on Free Radicals, or my definition of truly cool people.

I would be remiss if I didn't thank the restaurants where I wrote this pile of words. That would be Amarone (a delightful Italian restaurant in Hell's Kitchen) and the West Side Steakhouse (a terrific Midtown joint run by the affable Nick), and now this pretty awesome Austrian joint, Blaue Gans, run by a cool dude named Kurt. It would be safe to say that I wrote most of this while drinking. These places made sure I was fed.

And, of course, I thank my lovely wife, Elena, who saw very little of me on weekends and weeknights. (Something she might not have minded, but she was exceedingly patient with my deadline neurosis. I love her dearly.) My family deserves thanks, as I drifted in and out of conversations with them, always worried about unfinished chapters in between a two-show-a-day grind. They were stuck doing tougher things that I was able to escape. My mom deserves the most thanks, for sticking it out through a tough year and sticking with me.

Replace the idiocy of open-mindedness with shrewd judgmentalism

Triumph over liberal whiners

New York Times bestseller Greg Gutfeld offers his hilarious and insightful observations on our culture of artificial tolerance and phony outrage.

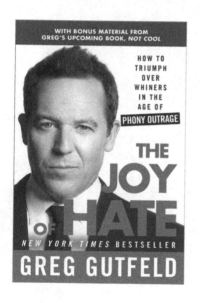

"*Greg Gutfeld is a sweet, hysterical, evil genius.*"
—ANN COULTER

"*Gutfeld is like Voltaire if Voltaire were actually funny.*"
—DENNIS MILLER

Printed in the United States
by Baker & Taylor Publisher Services